LIFE'S JOURNEYS

By the same author

Heritage of Israel

Wisdom of our Sages

The Development of Dualism in
    Pre-Talmudic and Talmudic Sources

Our Eternal Torah

Faith and Reason

Torah: The Tree Of Life

LIFE'S JOURNEYS

Rabbi Simon S. Silas, MA (Hons)

These are the journeys of the Children of Israel

Numbers 33:1

They journeyed and they encamped

Numbers 33:5

AESOP Jewish Studies
Oxford

AESOP Jewish Studies
An imprint of AESOP Publications
Martin Noble Editorial / AESOP
28 Abberbury Road, Oxford OX4 4ES, UK
www.aesopbooks.com

A catalogue record of this book is
available from the British Library.

First edition 2019

ISBN: 978-1-910301-63-0

Dedicated to my parents

The honour due to Parents is like the honour to God

Mekilta Exodus 20:12

To my wife

A virtuous woman is a crown to her husband

Proverbs 12:4

To my children and grandchildren

*Behold Children are a heritage of the Lord
and the fruit of the womb is his reward*

Psalms 127:3

PREFACE

THE TITLE of this book is *Life's Journeys*. The Bible describes in detail the journeys of the Children of Israel during their forty years in the desert until they reached the promised land. Every stage in their wanderings is mentioned with nothing more than: *'And they journeyed from one place and encamped in another.'*

The Rabbis state that the listing of the forty-two stops was to teach that each setting out from one place and encampment at another was important until they arrived in the Promised Land.

Human life is made up of a series of journeys, and every stage is an experience and purpose in the long history of life's challenges. But there are two journeys every person must undertake, a physical and a spiritual one; and whilst the physical one is essential there is also need for a spiritual one. The Torah as a guide enables us to attain both ends.

To be a Jew is to be on a journey and as a people we have never stood still. Judaism teaches that life is one long journey through time, and each movement and stoppage serves a higher purpose and better future.

The Torah as a moral compass enables us to go on life's journeys and face the trials and challenges that confront us. Commenting on the verse: 'For with wise advice you shall make your way' (Proverbs 24:6) a sage interpreted this as referring to the art of the captain of a ship. Rabbi Yohanan said: 'A man should ever be at the helm, like the captain on the ship on the lookout how good may best be achieved' (Leviticus Rabbah 21:4). This work *Life's Journeys* has been to me a labour of love. In this edited version of 'Sermons and Articles' delivered over the years to Sephardi congregations in North West London, I have quoted a treasury of statements from the Bible, Talmud, Midrash and Rabbinic literature in the belief that their ethical and spiritual themes offer wise counsel in our role as being the eternal people of God.

I hope that this work, filled with the wisdom of Scripture and Rabbinic commentaries, will inspire readers to a deeper understanding of our faith in God and direct them to face the challenges in 'life's journeys'.

Rabbi Simon S. Silas
London, 2019
1st print

ACKNOWLEDGEMENTS

I WOULD LIKE to thank the following people for their kind and generous support:

Louise and Simon Abraham
Solomon ben Atar
Benjamin Benarroch
Avraham Cohen
Michelle Dadoun
Albert ben Dahan
Reuben and Louise Elias
Menahem Haziza
Freddy Kelaty
David Kohali
Rabbi Dr Abraham Levy
Mark Lousky

I would like to express my special thanks to Janette Moore for typing the manuscript, continued help throughout the work and valuable suggestions; Judy Frankel for her creative input and invaluable assistance in the arduous task of proofreading and providing constructive advice; to my son-in-law Daniel Weisman for his invaluable assistance; and to Martin Noble for further editing, book and cover design and for arranging printing and distribution.

My personal thanks to my friends and supporters over the years and to the Young Israel congregation in North Netanya, Israel, where I first delivered these lectures as 'Articles'.

Wishing a complete Refuah Shlemah
to Rabbi Yehudah ben Preciada Benarroch.

ABOUT THE AUTHOR

RABBI SIMON SOLOMON SILAS studied for the Rabbinate at Manchester Talmudic College, England and the Ponovitch Yeshivah, Israel. He received his Rabbinical Semicha at the age of twenty-two from Rabbi Ovadiah Yosef, Member of the Supreme Rabbinical Court in Jerusalem; Rabbi Zvi Pesach Frank, Chief Rabbi of Jerusalem and the Rishon Lezion of Israel, Chief Rabbi Isaac Nissim.

He was Rabbi of Ohel David Synagogue, Golders Green, London (1961–63); spiritual leader to the Sephardi Congregation in Sydney, Australia (1963–80); he served as a Dayan at the Sydney Beth Din and President of the Rabbinical Association of Ministers in New South Wales and holds an MA (Hons) degree in Semitic studies from the university of Sydney, Australia. From 1980 to 1983 he was Senior Rabbi of Beehive Lane, United Synagogue, London.

Since 1983, Rabbi Silas has been actively identified in an honorary capacity with Sephardi congregations in north-west London and with rabbinical educational institutions in London. In his role as rabbi and educator he places great emphasis on Jewish learning and Torah values.

His published works are *Heritage of Israel, Wisdom of Our Sages, The Development of Dualism in Pre-Talmudic and Talmudic Sources, Our Eternal Torah, Faith and Reason* and *Torah: The Tree of Life.*

CONTENTS

Preface   vii
Acknowledgements   ix
About the author   x

PART I   15

BERESHIT
1   Bereshit – The Architect   17
2   Noach – The Dignity of Man   20
3   Lech Lecha – Loving Kindness   23
4   Lech Lecha – Individualism and Universalism   25
5   Vayyera – Justice and Mercy   28
6   Chayye Sarah – Faith and Duty   30
7   Toledoth – Two Elements within Man   33
8   Vayyetze – Protecting a Vow   35
9   Vayishlach – The Value of Reality   38
10 Vayyeshev – Suffering (1)   40
11 Miketz – Suffering (2)   43
12 Vayigash – The Character of Joseph   46
13 Vayyechi – Jewish Identity   48

SHEMOT
14 Shemot – Three Heroines   51
15 Va-ayra – The Significance of the Ten Plagues   54
16 Bo – The Spiritual Heritage   56
17 Beshalach – Not by Bread Alone   59
18 Yitro – Parents and Children   61
19 Mishpatim – The Hebrew Slave   63
20 Terumah – Praise and Thanksgiving   66
21 Tetzaveh – Make Me a Sanctuary   69
22 Ki Tissa – Accountability   71
23 Vayyakhel Pekudei – One Nation   74

VAYYIKRA
24 Vayyikra – The Heart of Man   77
25 Tzav – The Saving of Human Life   80
26 Shemini – Sanctification of the Body   83
27 Tazria – Metzora – Divine Providence   85
28 Acharei Mot – Kedoshim – Holiness Code   88
29 Emor – Arise and Give Light   90
30 Behar-Bechukosai – Exile and Redemption   93

BEMIDBAR
31 Bemidbar – In His Image   96
32 Naso – the Source of all Blessing   99
33 Beha'alotecha – Faith   102
34 Shelach Lecha – The Mission   105
35 Korach – Dangers of Self-Interest   108
36 Chukkat-Balak – Aaron the Peace Maker   111
37 Pinchas – Jeremiah's Message   114
38 Mattos-Massei – Illusory or Real Values   116

DEVARIM
39 Devarim – The Voice of Wisdom   119
40 Va'etchanan – Covenant between God and Israel   122
41 Ekev (1) – Recognising God's Goodness   125
42 Ekev (2) – Cleaving to God   127
43 Re'eh – Priest, Prophet and Sage   130
44 Shoftim – Ethics   134
45 Ki Thetze – The Eternal Message   137
46 Ki Thavo – Joy   139
47 Nitzavim – The True Leader   142
48 Vayyelech – Destiny of Man   144
49 Ha'azinu – Gratitude   146
50 Vezoth Ha-berachah – Partners in Creation   149

PART II   151

51 The Ten Commandments   153
52 Prophets and Their Prophecies   158
53 The Book of Job   164
54 Song of Songs   169
55 Pharisees and Sadducees   172
56 Babylonian Jewry   175
57 A Short History of the Marranos   178
58 A History of Jewish Liturgy   183
59 Reflections on Jewish History   186
60 The Halachic View of the Relationship between
   the Individual and Community   192
61 Dead Sea Scrolls – The Discovery and Importance   197
62 Moses: Man, Servant and Prophet   201
63 Haggadah   204
64 A Happy New Year   206

Bibliography   208
Biographical Notes   208

PART I

1

Bereshith

THE ARCHITECT

In the beginning God created the heaven and the earth

Genesis 1:1

THE FAITH OF ISRAEL is based on the opening verse of Genesis. Unlike other faiths, the Jew believes there is only one God and rejects all forms of paganism, polytheism and atheism. Whilst nowhere in the Bible is the belief in God questioned or speculated upon, but scattered over its teachings, we are told that He has no likeness nor can any image be made of Him (Exodus 20:4). The prophet Isaiah asks how idolators and pagans could mistake their man- made images for the omnipotent God. 'To whom can you liken God and what likeness can you attribute to Him?' (Isaiah 40:18).

God's power and wisdom find their expression in the works of creation, and the miracles found scattered throughout the *Tenach* (*Five Books of Moses, Prophets,* and *Writings*) highlight the incomparability of His existence. Unlike the teachings of Zoroaster – that there is a cosmic struggle between good and evil – or the pagan notion of demonic forces that wage war against the deities, the Bible proclaims God as the sole Power, the origin of all creation.

Our Sages were fully aware of man's limitations and the human mind's inability to comprehend the miracles that are around us at all times. The heavens above and the earth below are full of wonders but we are totally oblivious to the mystery that is found everywhere. The Psalmist expresses this wisdom: 'How abundant are Your works, O Lord, with wisdom You made them all.' (Psalm 104:24)

Again, 'The heavens declare the glory of God and the firmament relates the work of His hands.' (Psalm 19:2) In the *Midrash Temurah*, Chapter 3, Rabbi Akiva expressed this in the following manner: 'As a house implies a builder, a dress a weaver, a door a carpenter, so the world proclaims God as its Creator.'

The first-century Jewish philosopher Philo in his writings discusses God's relation to the world. 'Who can look upon statues or paintings without thinking at once of a sculptor or painter ... When he beholds hills and plains, the yearly seasons passing into each other and the whole firmament revolving in rhythmic order, must he not gain the conception of a Maker and Father, and Ruler also?' (Special Laws 1:6)

The First Principle of Judaism as expounded by Moses Maimonides is that of Faith, the belief in the existence of a Creator. This is a fundamental teaching of faith in an omnipotent God whose wisdom and power in creating an ant or bee is no less wondrous than in the making of the sun and its sphere.

Maimonides, in the beginning of his *Mishne Torah* writes: 'The fundamental of all fundamentals and the pillar of all forms of knowledge is the realisation that there is a First Being who brought all existing things into the world ... The knowledge of this truth is a positive command, as it is said: "I am the Lord your God."' (Exodus 20:2)

In addition to belief in God, there is the idea of Israel's chosenness, the concept of the election of the people of Israel as God's chosen people. In the covenant between God and Israel on Mount Sinai the nation accepted the Divine Law with a duty to live wholly in God's service.

According to Jewish teachings, the Jewish people were selected by God as his peculiar treasure and merited this election because of their special faithfulness to God. They were the only ones among the nations to accept the 'yoke of God's kingdom' at Mount Sinai and thereby merited God's special love.

Yet this concept of the 'chosen people' did not imply the rejection of the rest of mankind or monopoly of the divine love, for all human beings are God's children and have an equal claim upon His care and love. The election of Israel was an ethical charge, an obligation to live in accordance with the word and spirit of Sinai and to draw other nations closer to God and to righteousness.

In Jewish Rabbinic literature we are taught that God created man to sanctify His name in the world and that for the realisation of His plan and glory, the Jewish people have been chosen to be witnesses of His existence and Oneness. In the words of Isaiah, 'You are My witnesses, says the Lord, and My servant whom I have chosen.' (Isaiah 43:10)

2

Noach

THE DIGNITY OF MAN

*And the Lord saw that the wickedness of man was great
in the earth ... And the Lord said: I will blot out man
whom I have created from the face of the earth ...
and the earth was corrupt before God.*

Genesis 5:5, 7, 11

THE MISHNA in Sanhedrin 4:5 declares the uniqueness of man in the creation of the world by stating that he was created single to teach the sacredness of each individual in the divine plan of creation.

The Ramban, in his commentary at the beginning of Genesis, speaks of man's pre-eminence and difference from all other living creatures. His distinction, he says, lies in his being endowed with an intellect which grants him free will and the reasoning faculty to distinguish between right and wrong. Made in the divine image, man is further capable of becoming, as our Rabbis tell us, a partner with God in the continuing creation of the universe – 'shutaf imhakadosh baruch hu bemaseh bereshith' (Shabbat 10a).

It was this freedom of moral choice with the ability to distinguish between right and wrong, to obey or disobey, that singled him out from all creation. It was the dualism of his nature, born with a 'yetzer tov' and 'yetzer rah' to do good or evil, that made him little lower than the angels.

In ancient non-Jewish sources, such as Persian dualism, life was considered as a continuous struggle between the physical and spiritual, the body and the soul. The body was considered as the source of all evil with the soul being in constant conflict within man. The Qumran community, who lived in the Judean desert, on the northwest shore of the Dead Sea, also believed in this dualistic philosophy, where the spirits of truth and error were in continuous conflict and in the ways of one of the two spirits men walked.

In Rabbinic literature, on the other hand, every person is a composite of body and soul, responsible for his actions, whether for good or bad. The Rabbis in Sanhedrin 91a and b record a discussion between the Emperor Antoninus and Rabbi Judah the Prince. Antoninus said to him: 'A person's body and soul are able to excuse themselves from final judgement, by the body saying it is the soul that has sinned, since from the day it has departed from me I have been unable to sin. The soul, on the other hand, blames the body that has sinned, for from the day the soul has departed it is unable to sin.'

Rabbi Judah replied: 'I will give you a parable – to what can this matter be compared? To a king who had a splendid orchard which contained beautiful figs, and placed two guards, one lame and the other blind, to protect them. One day the lame one said to the blind one: "I see beautiful figs in the orchard. Come, mount on my shoulders and together we will bring down the figs and eat them." The blind one agreed, brought down the figs, and together they ate them. Some time later, the king came and asked: "Where are those beautiful figs?" The lame one said: "Do I have any feet with which to take the figs?" The blind one then said: "Do I have any eyes with which to see where the figs are?"' What did the king do? He mounted the lame one on the back of the blind one and judged them as one unit. 'So too', said Rabbi Judah, 'on the Day of Judgement, the Holy One, blessed be He, will bring the soul and the body together and judge them as one unit.'

Human life is sacred in all its forms and needs. It is for a reason that our Sages opposed any form of asceticism or self-harm. Similarly, a Nazarite was considered a sinner because he undertook to abstain from wine during the period of his Nazariteship. Maimonides, at the beginning of his Yad HaChazakah, writes: 'If a man says: "Since passion and honour are evil traits to have in this world, I will separate myself from them in great measure or will not eat meat, nor drink wine, nor marry, nor have a nice home, nor wear nice clothes, but will cover myself in sackcloth," this is also wrong and whoever continues in such a manner is called a sinner' (Hilchot Deot 3:1). We thus learn that denying oneself things which are permitted is not just wrong but contrary to the Torah's view of taking proper care of one's body.

Let us conclude by quoting the Psalmist on man's uniqueness in all God's creation. 'You have made him slightly lower than the angels and crowned him with honour and dignity' (8:6). Indeed, man is the only creature called upon to do his duty, morally free, possessed of spirit, and granted freedom of choice to answer to God for the use to which he was put into this world.

3

Lech Lecha

LOVINGKINDNESS

And God said to Abraham ... And I will make
you a great nation; and be thou a blessing.

Genesis 12:1, 3

THE PATRIARCH ABRAHAM has been portrayed in Rabbinic literature as an example of one whose fame spread and who was granted the privilege of blessing all who came into contact with him (Genesis Rabbah 39:12). Renowned for his hospitality to strangers, he directed his entire life in service to others. Recovering from his circumcision, the Bible informs us of his eagerness to provide a meal to passers-by and though offering to grant them 'a morsel of bread' gives them a sumptuous meal. The Midrash Tanchuma derived from this a moral lesson. 'Good men perform more than they promise, whilst the wicked say more than they perform' (Vayyera).

Legend has it that Abraham's house was built on the highway, and in order not to inconvenience visitors he made four entrances to his home. It is no wonder that our Sages characterise him as one filled with human kindness, *gemilut chasadim*.

The Vilna Gaon once explained that there are three principal domains in man's life: three fundamentals, which make up the whole of human existence. They are: the Divine, the self, and our fellow man. However, mankind views them quite differently. The first is the immediate interest a person has for himself. The second is the worship of God and the need to serve Him. The third is the desire to give and assist others.

Though worship of God, according to the Vilna Gaon, should rightfully precede acts of kindness, our Sages tell us that the Holy One, Blessed be He, prefers acts of kindness to His honour. The following story illustrates this. Rabbi Yochanan ben Zakkai was once walking from Jerusalem accompanied by Rabbi Joshua. When Rabbi Joshua noticed the remains of the ruined Temple, he said: 'Alas, this place where Jews brought their offerings to God to atone for their sins is now destroyed.' Rabbi Yochanan replied: 'My son, don't be distressed, we still have another means of atonement which is even greater, that of acts of kindness, as it is written: "For acts of kindness I desired and not sacrifice" (Hosea 6:6)' (Avoth de Rabbi Natan 4).

An excellent example of loving-kindness is illustrated in the following Talmudic passage. 'Rabbi Huna ben Hanina, commenting on the verse "After the Lord your God shall you walk" (Deuteronomy 13:5), asks: "Is it possible for a mortal man to emulate the Divine Presence? Has it not been said: 'For the Lord your God is a consuming fire?' (ibid. 4:24)." This can be explained as that we should emulate the attributes of the Holy One, blessed be He. Just as He clothes the naked, you too should clothe the naked; as the Holy One, blessed be He, visits the sick, so you too should visit the sick; as the Holy One, blessed be He, comforts mourners, you too should comfort mourners; as the Holy One, blessed be He, buries the dead, you too should bury the dead' (T. Sotah 14a).

Though financial assistance is meritorious, yet acts of kindness are superior to alms-giving in three ways. First Tzedakah is done with one's money, whilst Gemiluth Chasadim are furthered by both body and mind, as they are generally involved in extending a helping hand to our fellow men. Secondly, alms-giving is exclusively directed to the poor, whilst acts of kindness apply to both rich and poor. Thirdly, money can help the living only, whilst acts of kindness can be performed for the dead as well (Sukkah 49b).

Whilst the mitzvah of doing charitable acts is incumbent upon us all, it was of even greater importance to treat the less fortunate with due care and tenderness. The Gemarah relates that Rabbi Yannai saw a man give charity to a needy person publicly in an unbecoming manner. The Rabbi said to him: 'It had been better that you had not given him in this manner and put him to shame' (Hagigah 5a).

Let us conclude with the two following quotations of our teachers. The prophet Micah said: 'Man, He has told you what is good, for what does the Lord require of you: but to do justly, and to love mercy, and to walk humbly with your God?' (6:8). Simon the Just said: 'Upon three things the world is based: upon the Torah, upon Divine Service and upon the practice of lovingkindness' (Pirkei Avoth 1:2).

4

Lech Lecha

INDIVIDUALISM AND UNIVERSALISM

*And the Lord said to Abraham: 'Go you out of your country
and birthplace ... and I will make of you a great nation
and you shall be a blessing ... and in you shall
be blessed all the families of the earth'*

Genesis 12:1–3

ABRAHAM was chosen by God to be the bearer of a message to mankind. He was to spread the name of God upon earth and teach the way of serving God by doing righteousness and justice. The Midrash says that when God spoke at the beginning of 'Let there be light' He had Abraham in mind: for it was through him that the world would be brought out of darkness into spiritual light.

As the founder of the Jewish people, he would bear the torch of enlightenment to teach the belief in one God, Creator of all things. In his old age, he wandered from place to place, constantly travelling, never complaining and working towards the fulfilment of his goals. But as the Parashah informs us, these journeys were not all spiritual ascents. After arriving in the land of Canaan, there was a famine in the country which led him to go down to Egypt. There, his wife Sarah was taken by Pharaoh, but miraculously was saved from harm because of a debilitating skin disease. On his return to Eretz Yisrael, he underwent further trials, but his faith in God did not waver. Our Rabbis say that Abraham underwent ten tests and, no matter how difficult the circumstances, never abandoned his faith in God.

But the call to have faith in one God, monotheism, and to be a blessing, was not one of pure nationalism. Whilst his teachings were directed to the Jewish people, his descendants, yet they brought a message to all humanity. The command 'You shall be a blessing and through you shall be blessed all the families of the earth' made it clear that his teachings also carried a universal message.

It is true that there are commandments and teachings which are only directed to the Jewish people. For example: kashrut, Shabbat, and the observance of the festivals did not apply to others. On the other hand, the injunction concerning Abraham: 'I have known him to the end that he may command his children and his household after him to keep the way of the Lord, to do righteousness and justice' was to be an influence for good which would apply to the whole of humanity.

Let me explain this more clearly. The practice of Jewish teachings can be divided into two halves. The first is *'ben adam lemakom'* – duties in our relationship to God. The second is *'ben adam lechavero'* – duties in our relationship to our fellow men. As far as the former is concerned, the observance of kashrut, Shabbat and the laws of holiness are to be observed by Jews because God willed it to be so. But the laws concerning murder, stealing, bearing false witness and other rules about relationships do not apply just to Jews but to all peoples. These are essentially humanitarian laws completely understandable even without God's command. Yet, Judaism states that the sanction for these laws is by the will of God.

One of the characteristics of Jewish culture is that of compassion. Whilst the Bible draws our attention to this in the thirteen attributes of God's nature as we read in Exodus 34:6,7 'the Lord, the Lord God, merciful and gracious, long-suffering and abundant in goodness and truth, keeping mercy unto the thousandth generation, forgiving iniquity and transgression and sin', this idea of imitating the attributes of God became characteristic of the Jewish way of life. They regulate our relationship with our fellow men and would also determine one's relationship with humanity.

Indeed, the relationship of man with his neighbour of whatever race is the standard of a civilised society and fundamental to the seven precepts set out in Chapter Nine of Genesis. These *'mitzvot bnei Noah'* – the seven fundamental laws given to the children of Noah – constitute what one may call 'Natural Religion'. It is worthwhile to enumerate them: 1. The establishment of courts of justice. 2. Prohibition of blasphemy. 3. Idolatry. 4. Incest. 5. Bloodshed. 6. Robbery. 7. Eating flesh from a living animal.

All these laws are essentially humanitarian commands required of all civilised people, and whilst Jews were given six hundred and thirteen commandments on Mount Sinai, these seven precepts were given to all nations and highlight man's precious heritage.

5

Vayyera

JUSTICE AND MERCY

And the Lord said: Shall I hide from Abraham that which I am doing?
For I have known him, to the end that he may command his children and
his household after him, that they keep the way
of the Lord to do righteousness and justice.

Genesis 18:17, 19

ABRAHAM, the founder of the Jewish people, was reared in a home where idolatry was practised. At an early age, he reached the belief that the universe was the work of a creator, a Supreme Being, who is the God of righteousness. In teaching others the folly of idolatry, he presents a doctrine which needs to be emphasised even today, that of the knowledge of the one true God.

In Aggadic literature, Abraham is compared to a bottle of perfume which, when opened, spreads around its sweet fragrance. Because of his proselytising activities the Rabbis regarded him as the father of all proselytes, who are given the name Abraham.

In Vayyera, the greatness of the patriarch Abraham is shown, for God reveals to him the wickedness of Sodom and Gomorrah and Abraham's appeal to save the cities (Genesis 18:23–33). The reason for revealing this to Abraham was so that he could continue to command his children to do righteousness and justice.

In his dialogue with God, Abraham intercedes on behalf of the inhabitants of Sodom, displaying the nobility of his character. Commenting on the word '*vayyigash*' – he 'drew near' – Rashi explains that he drew near to argue, appease and pray on behalf of Sodom. In this dialogue he pleads not just for the wicked people there but also for the righteous in whose merit the cities should be saved.

Abraham begins his address to God with the words: 'Will you indeed sweep away the righteous with the wicked?' (ibid. 23). His plea not to punish the just with the wicked, if only ten just men were found, shows that even the wicked inhabitants of Sodom were his brothers. In his pleas for the people, Abraham, whilst arguing on their behalf, is aware that God is always ready to pardon if there are sufficient righteous men who could save the city.

On the verse: 'If I find in Sodom fifty righteous within the city' (ibid. 26), Ibn Ezra explains 'within the city' to mean that these righteous have an influence which can have an effect on others. Unfortunately, Abraham had failed to find even ten good men and the fate of the city was sealed.

It is interesting that Abraham, in his plea for the inhabitants, begins his address to God with the words: 'Shall not the judge of all the earth do justly?' (ibid. 25). To the patriarch, the essential quality of the Almighty is 'justice' and for God to act unjustly would be contrary to the rule of human conduct. In Jewish thought, justice is fundamental and essential for the survival of society as a whole. In the Book of Deuteronomy, we are told: 'Justice, justice you shall follow, that you may live' (16:20). If one considers the cause of so much evil in the world, the answer would undoubtedly be the lack of justice. No wonder then that justice holds a central place in the Jewish world view.

In Rabbinic literature, God is described as drawing on the two attributes of lawfulness and mercy (see Maimonides, Guide for the Perplexed, 3:5) and it is man's obligation to imitate Him by acting on the principles of justice and mercy. It is in the light of these two ethical principles that we can understand the following Midrashic comment: 'Abraham spoke before the Holy One, blessed be He: If You wish the world to exist then there must not be strict justice, but if You wish strict justice, then the world cannot endure.' (Genesis Rabbah 49:9).

Let us conclude with the following declaration which God daily pronounces: 'May it be My will that My mercy may subdue My anger and that My mercy prevail over My attribute of justice.' (Berachoth 7a).

6

Chayyei Sarah

FAITH AND DUTY

And Abraham was old, when stricken in age;
and the Lord blessed Abraham in all things

Genesis 24:1

ABRAHAM, the first of the Patriarchs, was the pioneer of the monotheistic faith and founder of the Jewish people. But what kind of person was he and why was he chosen to be the father of many nations? Why was he singled out and charged with the divine mission of founding a kingdom of priests and a holy nation? The Torah tells us little of the early life of Abraham and one needs to turn to a Midrash to justify Abraham's selection.

Midrash Rabbah traces the failures of mankind, until Abraham appeared, into three stages. The first was with Adam who failed to live up to his role as one chosen to bring redemption to mankind. Noach, ten generations later, was a righteous and good man, but did not involve himself in returning his generation to a belief in God. Ten generations later Abraham appeared, an iconoclast prepared to fight for the belief in one God even to the extent of martyring himself (Genesis Rabbah 39:5).

The Ramban in his commentary on the Torah adduces the Almighty's choice of Abraham to his noble acts. He writes: 'The real reason for this choice was that the Chaldeans had persecuted Abraham for his faith in God which led him by divine word to the land of Canaan. Unlike his experience in Chaldea, where he had been despised and reviled, he would rally others to a belief in the true God.' But, asks the Ramban, if Abraham had been chosen because of his campaign against idolatry, why does the Torah not record this? He answers: 'The Torah did not wish to elaborate on idolatry and dwell on the issues Abraham faced with the Chaldeans and their idolatrous practices.'

Rashi explains that Abraham was commanded by God to leave his place of birth and travel in order to spread His renown in the world. He quotes Midrash Tanchumah: 'A bottle of perfume standing in a corner would not be enjoyed by others, but when opened, its scent would spread abroad. Similarly, in your travels, the fragrance of your personality will draw people far and near to serve Me. Moreover, in changing your place of residence I will make of you a great nation.'

Before Abraham was called upon to become the founder of the Jewish nation, there were others like Enosh and Noach who believed in one God. What distinguished Abraham from the others was that his belief in God was more than an idea, and involved a strong sense of duty, a call to service and a willingness to sacrifice everything for his faith.

In the story of Sodom, we see Abraham pleading with God on behalf of its inhabitants. Disturbed by the loss of human life, even for sinners, he pleads with the Almighty: 'Shall not the Judge of all the earth do justly?' In his intercession on behalf of the population, Abraham expresses his concern for others. In the sublime plea he makes on behalf of the doomed city, Abraham shows that the principles of justice need to be tempered with mercy.

Let us quote the Zohar on Abraham's conduct which marked him out for his spiritual destiny. Commenting on the verse: 'And Abraham drew near and said: "Will You also destroy the righteous and the wicked?"' Rabbi Judah asked: 'Who has seen a father as compassionate as Abraham?' Regarding Noach, it is stated: 'And God said to Noach, the end of all flesh is come before Me ... and behold I will destroy his creations.' Yet Noach held his peace and said nothing. Whereas Abraham, as soon as the Holy One, blessed be He, said to him: 'The cry of Sodom and Gemorrah is great and their sin is very grievous,' he immediately 'drew near and asked: "Will you destroy the righteous with the wicked?"'

Solomon Dubov – explaining Abraham's question: 'Will you destroy the righteous with the wicked?' – points out that Abraham prayed that God should deliver even the wicked for the sake of the righteous; but if his prayer were of no avail then at least He should save the righteous.

What emerges from the dialogue between Abraham and God is the moral responsibility of the righteous to intercede on behalf of others even when they are corrupt and sinners.

It is interesting that earlier the Torah informs us of the reason for which God chose Abraham to be the father of the Jewish nation. 'For I know him to the end that he will command his children and his household after him, that they may keep the way of the Lord, to do righteousness and justice' (Genesis 18:19). This doctrine of righteousness and justice has continued throughout the ages to be the guiding principle of Jewish life, a duty enunciated by the prophet Isaiah: 'The work of righteousness shall be peace; and the effect of righteousness, quietness and confidence forever' (32:17).

7

Toledoth

TWO ELEMENTS WITHIN MAN

And Esau said to Jacob: 'Let me swallow, I pray you, some of the red pottage; for I am faint ... Behold, I am about to die, and what profit shall the birthright do to me?'

Toledoth 25:30, 32

THE GEMARA in Baba Batra 16b states that the sale of the birthright from Esau to Jacob occurred on the day of Abraham's death and instead of respecting his grandfather's day of mourning he publicly committed a number of sins. At a time when people from all over stood and lamented: 'Woe to the world that has lost its leader' (ibid. 91b), Esau went about his evil ways unconcerned with his family's bereavement.

The Hebrew word *'Haleiteni'* which means 'swallow' or 'pour' implies an animal-like voracity with an impulsiveness to receive something immediately. Again, when Esau uses the expression in verse 31 *'Anochi holeich lamut'* 'I am at the point of death', this is nothing other than an exaggeration of a hungry person unable to control his desires and reflects upon his character.

The birthright, which was a spiritual inheritance handed down from Abraham, carried with it a mission of divine service. Esau, by his physical gratification and removal from normal human values, showed that he was unsuitable to hold on to this privilege of being a priest. His impulsive nature, divorced from moral and spiritual ideals, showed that he was not worthy to be the heir of Abraham's spiritual inheritance

The Bible records, in the first chapter of Genesis, the creation of man: 'And God said: 'Let us make man in our image, after our likeness' (v.26). In the second chapter we are told that: 'God formed man of the dust of the ground and breathed into his nostrils the breath of life and man became a living soul' (ibid. 2:7). We thus see that man's life is composed of two elements, a body and a soul: the body being the product of the earth whilst the soul being a spiritual entity. Man was therefore made out of both the earthly, physical world, whilst his soul from the Divine spirit. The uniqueness of man, says the Zohar, is that his soul is part of God's essence as it were, which elevates him above the animal kingdom. As man is composed of these two elements by the nature of their origins, they are part of his very being.

The body being physical will stop at nothing to procure what it desires. The soul, however, brings, with its partnership with the body, a spiritual dimension that enables him to use the faculty of thinking, speech and action in the service of God.

It is only natural that there arise in every human being inner conflicts between these two elements, conflicts which are obstacles in his search for happiness and peace of mind.

This inner conflict, the struggle between the physical and spiritual, can be resolved in one or two ways. One is the total defeat of either the bodily desires or soul-like discrimination by granting it full control over the body. The second approach is that of co-operation between the two elements.

Judaism teaches that the body and soul need to collaborate. Both asceticism and hedonism are wrong and it is through the middle path that one can achieve inner peace and contentment. Indeed, human life, if it is to be properly lived, must combine the physical with the spiritual, satisfying the needs of both parts of man's nature. Unfortunately, Esau, as we saw earlier, showed in his general behaviour that his physical gratification and murderous tendencies deprived him of the birthright which otherwise was his and which led to a hatred between him and Jacob that remains to this very day.

In Jewish tradition, on the other hand, we are called upon to take proper care of our body supplying its needs as well as providing for the soul, which is invested with sacredness and moral freedom.

8

Vayyetze

PROTECTING A VOW

And Isaac sent Jacob away and he went to Padan Aram
unto Laban ... the brother of Rebekah.

Genesis 28:5

And Jacob went out from Beer Sheva and went unto Haran.

ibid. 10

JACOB, fleeing from his brother Esau and his birthplace, is on his
journey to Haran. There alone he has a remarkable experience. As the
sun sets, he lies down to sleep and dreams of a ladder standing on the
earth, the top of it reaching to heaven, with angels ascending and
descending upon it. God then speaks to him and promises him the
blessings of his ancestors Abraham and Isaac, that the land upon which
he lies would be given to him and his descendants. Furthermore, he is
promised divine protection that he will return to his ancestral home.
Jacob, on awakening from his sleep, vows: 'If God will be with me, and
will protect me on the way that I go, and will give me bread to eat and
raiment to put on, so that I return to my father's house in peace, then
shall the Lord be my God' (ibid. 20, 21).

Our commentators raise a number of questions to Jacob's reaction
to God's promises. Firstly, was it right for him to doubt God's promise
that the land upon which he lay would belong to his descendants?
Secondly, should he have conditioned his loyalty to God if he would
receive divine protections and material benefits?

Isaac Abravanel, a fifteenth-century philosopher and statesman,
expresses these problems by asking: 'How could Jacob say: "If God
will be with me and keep me and give me bread to eat and raiment to
put on then shall the Lord be my God", implying that if God did not
grant him these things he would not serve Him?'

35

Let us consider Rashi's view on this problem. He explains that what Jacob meant was his concern that away from his parental home and during the period he spent with his uncle Lavan, he might not be worthy of God's promises. Living among idolators, there was danger that he might deviate from the moral and ethical way of life he lived until now. The Midrash Rabbah explains this by stating: '*Ein havtacha letzadik ba'olam hazeh*' – 'there is no promise for the righteous in this world'. The Rabbis mean by this that the promise of protection to the righteous is conditional on their behaviour and way of life. Jacob then did not doubt God's promise to him but doubted his ability to withstand the dangers that would confront him and thereby not be worthy to receive those promises. He therefore vowed that if divine providence would assist him to overcome those dangers and not be corrupted he would fulfil his vow.

In Pirkei Avot we are told: 'Do not believe in yourself until the day of your death' (2:5). In this statement we are reminded that even if by nature one is good, there is a need constantly to be on guard against falling into sin throughout one's life. The Talmud cites the case of a Sage who held the office of High Priest for eighty years and then lapsed into becoming a Sadducee.

Maimonides, in his commentary on the Mishna, says: 'Let a man not neglect the opportunity to do good again and again in order that he fix righteousness in his soul. Let him not be over confident stating: "This virtue I have already mastered successfully, it can never leave me." There is always the possibility that it may.'

In Midrash Shocher Tov, we are told: 'The Holy One, blessed be He, does not call a tzaddik a saint until he has been put into the grave. Why? Because all the days of his life he is beset by the evil inclination and God does not trust him until the day of his death.' The moral of this teaching is that one should not be over-confident that although today one has lived honestly and properly one will do so tomorrow as well. Every day brings with it new and unprepared challenges.

Rabbi Israel Salanter, founder of the Mussar Movement (Ethical Culture Movement) compares a human being to a bird. He writes that just as a bird will soar ever higher only as long as it vigorously beats its wings but will fall and descend to earth once it stops, so too is it with a person. So long as he is actively engaged in constantly refining his character and self-improvement he will rise ever higher in his spiritual attainment. When, however, he discontinues his efforts, and slackens in his quest, he will begin to fall from his previously high status of spiritual attainment.

Based on the text: 'You shall not try the Lord' (Deuteronomy 6:16), the Gemara in Shabbat 32a says one is advised not to stand in a place of danger in reliance upon a miracle to save him but should do everything possible to overpower the evil inclination. So, returning to Jacob, he never cast doubt on God's words nor showed lack of faith but wished to prove himself worthy of the promise made to him. This is the message that we take from Jacob's vow. Life may be a hard struggle with success and failure and with temptation always before us, but with faith and courage we will be worthy of the divine blessings.

9

Vayyishlach

THE VALUE OF REALITY

And Jacob said: 'I am not worthy of all the mercies and by all the truth which You have done to Your servant; for with a staff I passed over this Jordan and now I am become two camps.'

Genesis 32:10, 11

THE PARSHA opens with Jacob sending messengers to his brother Esau in the hope that, after a lapse of twenty years, his brother's anger had cooled. But the emissaries return with the evil tidings: 'We came to your brother Esau but he is coming to meet you and with four hundred men' (ibid. 7).

How did Jacob react to this news? What steps did he take to safeguard himself and those accompanying him? Our Sages say that he adopted three ways to meet the danger ahead. Firstly, he turned to God in prayer; secondly, he hoped to appease Esau through gifts; lastly, he prepared himself to fight. Jacob in his prayer speaks of the endless kindnesses the Almighty has bestowed upon him. He recalls how, as a wanderer fleeing from Esau twenty years earlier, he was unworthy of the benefits conferred on him, 'for with my staff I crossed the Jordan and now I am become two camps'. In great humility and gratitude Jacob declares his unworthiness and throws himself on God's mercies.

The Ramban in his commentary states that the pious person is constantly aware that nothing he has is rightly his and is consciously aware of the gifts God daily confers on him.

But the question must be asked: Surely Jacob must have believed that he was a righteous man? In his message to Esau did he not state: 'I have sojourned with Laban' (ibid. 32), where the Midrash explains that the Hebrew word for sojourn is *'garti'* which equals *'Taryag'* – 613, meaning though I have sojourned with Laban, I have observed the 613 commandments? So why was Jacob afraid? Moreover, did not God promise him His protection when he was on his way to Haran? (ibid.

38

28:15). Many of our Rabbinical commentators indeed question how Jacob could doubt God's fulfilment of the divine promise.

Varied are the answers offered by our Sages. The Midrash Tanhuma says: 'Such is the character of pious men, though the Holy One, blessed be He, promises them His protection, that they fear they may have sinned in some way and thereby forfeited Divine protection.' In other words, the righteous understand that the promises granted them by Divine grace are conditional, depending on their not becoming soiled by sin. A similar idea is expressed in Midrash Bereshit Rabbah 76:2; 'There is no guarantee for the righteous in this world as it depends on their conduct in life.'

The Abravanel offers a further explanation of Jacob's apprehension. He explains that Jacob's fear of Esau was not due to his weakness of faith and trust in God. But his fear was like that of the real hero who goes to battle aware of the dangers that lie ahead. Jacob's fears were based on Esau possibly killing him and his wives and children. It is the fear which even the bravest of heroes recognises only too well. The fifteenth-century Talmudist, Isaac Arama, in his *Akedat Yitzchak*, writes that whilst the Psalmist says: 'Behold the eye of the Lord is towards those that revere Him, to save their soul from death' (33:18, 19) nevertheless human initiative is called for, and the lack of it where necessary const-itutes a sin. The Midrash offers yet another reason for Jacob's fear: his great anguish at the thought that he may be forced to kill Esau.

We thus see that like Jacob, a pious righteous person whilst always conscious of God's blessings in all that he receives does not take life for granted. The duty of self-help, of the need to do everything possible by one's own efforts to extricate oneself from trouble and danger, is the proper way to receive Divine favour.

10

Vayyeshev

SUFFERING (1)

How long O Lord shall I cry and you will not hear?

Habakkuk 1:2

Awake, why sleepest You, O Lord? Why do You hide Your face
and forget our affliction and our oppression?

Psalm 44:b22, 25

AFTER undergoing many ordeals in his life, Jacob wished to settle down to a life of peace. Whilst at his parents' home, Esau wished to kill him, forcing him to go to his uncle, Lavan. During his twenty years he was deceived by his uncle many times which led him to flee from Lavan. Following that, he was shamed by the rape of his daughter Dinah, struggled with a divine being and overcame the danger of being killed by Esau.

Finally, he returned to the land of Canaan, desiring to seek a life of tranquility, but this was not to be. Commenting on the verse: 'And Jacob settled in the land of his father's sojournings, in the land of Canaan', Rashi quotes the following *Midrash Rabbah*: 'Jacob wished to dwell in peace but there sprang upon him the troubles of Joseph. The righteous seek tranquility, but the Holy One, blessed be He, says: "Are the righteous not satisfied with what awaits them in the world to come but they seek to dwell in peace also in this world?" (84:3).' Following his desire for a quiet life, the Rabbis inform us that the anguish of Joseph's kidnapping came upon him.

The question one needs to ask is: Why are the good and righteous not permitted to enjoy, after years of toil and hardships, the right to a peaceful life? Why do they need to undergo further pain and suffering? There are no easy solutions to this problem, especially when we believe in a kind and benevolent God. In the Bible, of which two examples have been offered in our opening texts, the problem of reconciling

God's wisdom with His love is a struggle not easily resolved. The entire book of Job deals with this dilemma of how God's judgement can be reconciled with the idea of mercy. One answer is that a person during his lifetime undergoes numerous experiences. It was therefore necessary for Jacob not to expect a life of ease and comfort but to engage in the events and affairs that would confront him and his family. Each day would bring with it new challenges and Jacob would need to deal with them with courage and strength of character.

Let us consider some other views expressed by our Sages on this subject. One explanation is that suffering may be a punishment for misdeeds. The Talmud states: 'There is no death without sin and no suffering without transgression' (Sabbath 55b). Man is given the power to choose: 'I have set before you life and death, the blessing and the curse, therefore choose life' (Deuteronomy 32:19). If man suffers, there is good reason. Many are the modes of punishment for transgression, such as suffering, disease and exile. On the other hand, suffering may be a test of loyalty or to purify and refine human character. Rav Huna, a second century Babylonian scholar, found the doctrine of suffering to be a sign of God's favour. In the words of the prophet Isaiah: 'Whom the Lord is fond of, He crushes with suffering' (53:10). In this, the Sages refused to deny that evil can occur without sin. In the book of Psalms, we read: 'Happy is the man whom you chastise, O Lord, and teaches out of Your Law.' (92:12) Here the psalmist calls such a person 'Happy'. Rava, another Babylonian Sage, said: 'If a person sees that afflictions befall him, let him scrutinise his deeds. If he examines and finds nothing let him be sure that these are chastenings of love. For it is said: "For whom the Lord loves, He corrects"' (Berachot 5a).

Rabbi S. R. Hirsch offers us a further insight into the importance of sufferings. He writes: 'Understand your sufferings and give thanks for them as the truest gift of a father, for they are sent to train and test. As training they teach you to know yourself and to know God, His power and goodness to live in His service. As a test they promote inner purity and make you strong in acknowledging the unending gifts you have received from him' (Horeb Ch. 1).

It is perhaps in this light that one can understand Jacob's meeting and wrestling with the angel. In the struggle at night with Esau's guardian angel, Jacob had to face the reasons for his running away from home, and why Esau wished to meet him with four hundred men. It was only after this wrestling and facing up to the cause of his sufferings that Jacob was able to meet Esau and able finally to part from him in peace.

The renowned second century author of the Zohar puts forward the view that nothing of importance is achievable without suffering. 'The Holy One, blessed be He, gave Israel three precious gifts, and all of them were attainable only through suffering. These are: Torah, the land of Israel, and the world to come' (Berachot 5a).

Perhaps in this light one may understand why Jacob was denied the peace he sought; for in order to achieve his mission in life he needed to undergo further sacrifice and suffering for his future generations and for the destiny of the Jewish people.

11

Mikketz

SUFFERING (2)

The brothers took Joseph and cast him into the pit;
the pit was empty, no water was in it

Genesis 37:24

Then Pharaoh sent and called Joseph, and they brought
him hastily out of the dungeon

ibid. 41:14

THE PARSHIOT Vayyeshev and Mikketz centre upon the life of Joseph and the dangers he encountered. As a result of the jealousy of his brothers, he is thrown into a pit, then sold as a slave into the house of Potiphar where he is falsely charged by his master's wife and once again placed into a prison. It is natural to read of these events as part of biblical narrative but what did Joseph feel in those thirteen years of adversity? Where were his dreams of greatness and his belief in God? The Torah does not answer these questions but he is only referred to as 'the righteous one', indicating that no matter what he underwent his strong faith in God was unwavering.

In the words of the biblical commentator Isaac Abravanel: 'Joseph saw the sale of his brothers as the work of providence and that they were unwittingly chosen as God's instrument in carrying out the design of providence.'

In Deuteronomy 22: 6, 7, the Torah forbids us to take a mother-bird when she is sitting on her eggs or young. One must send away the mother-bird and only then is it permitted to take her eggs or young. If one does so, the Torah promises the person 'it will be good for you and will prolong your days'. The Talmud relates that a Sage observed a child climbing a tree to gather eggs from a nest in obedience to his father's command and the Bible's ordinance. Coming down the ladder, the child fell and died. The shock of the death of this innocent child who dutifully followed the Torah's two commands of honouring the father's wish and sending the mother-bird from her nest led him to proclaim: 'There is no judge and no justice!' Rabbi Akiva, however, explained that the promise of goodness and longevity refers to the world to come which is wholly good and all-abiding (Kiddushin 39b).

The Midrash, on the other hand, interprets the concept: 'And it will be good for you and will prolong your days' as meaning that the reward for the fulfilment of this precept is to have children, i.e. by your sending the mother-bird away, your longevity will reside in the blessing of descendants (Tanchuma).

The problem of reconciling God's goodness with human affliction and suffering goes back to the beginning of history. The saintly Job, robbed of his possessions and bereft of his children, retained faith in the greatness of God by exclaiming 'Shall we accept the good from God and not the bad also?' (Job 2:10). Further on in this book, Job says: 'Though God slays me, still will I trust Him' (ibid13:15).

The importance of enduring faith in God's goodness is one of the great lessons of religion. At times the hardships we undergo in life may prove beneficial as the following story illustrates. Rabbi Akiva had a favourite motto: 'Whatever the Merciful One does is for the best' ('*Kol derachmana avid letav avid*'.) Once, he was travelling and arrived at a certain place at the end of the day and looked for a night's lodging at an inn but was refused a place. Tired, he said: 'Whatever the Merciful One does is for the best' and spent the night in the forest. He had with him a rooster, an ass and a lamp. Later that night, a gust of wind came and blew out the lamp, a weasel came and ate the rooster and a lion killed the ass. After all that he said: 'Whatever the Merciful One does is for the best.' The next morning, Rabbi Akiva entered the town only to learn that a band of robbers had come there and killed all the people there. He then said: 'Had I stayed in the town or had my lamp and animals been alive, I too would have shared their fate. All that the Merciful One does is for the best' (Berachot 60b).

Similarly, in the life of Joseph, one can understand how adversity and suffering were stepping stones to his later success and greatness.

It is related that the saintly Rabbi Levi Yitzchak of Berdichev wrote in his last testament before he died amidst the flames of the Warsaw ghetto: 'I believe in the God of Israel even though he has done everything to destroy my belief in Him. I believe in His laws even though I cannot justify His ways.'

We will never be able to fathom God's purpose in things that happen in life. But the message one takes is that we are in the hands of God and in good fortune or in ill fortune, He knows what is best for us. Yes, in the words of Rabbi Akiva, who himself died as a martyr, 'All that the Merciful One does is for the best.'

12

Vayigash

THE CHARACTER OF JOSEPH

And Joseph said: 'I am Joseph, your brother, whom you sold into Egypt.
And now be not grieved, nor angry that you sold me here;
for God did send me before you to preserve life.'

Genesis 45: 4, 50

THE STORY of Joseph and his rise to greatness is well worth a study. Throughout his difficulties and sufferings, he possessed he gift of winning the favour of those with whom he came into contact. Though sold as a slave by his brothers and taken down to Egypt he was bought by Potiphar, an officer of Pharaoh. There he gained the good opinion of his master who 'appointed him overseer in the house, and over all that he had' (ibid. 39:5). Following this, Potiphar's wife had him imprisoned on a false charge, and whilst there won the goodwill and respect of the keeper of the prison and fellow prisoners.

Throughout those years in Egypt Joseph, though living in foreign surrounding where he had every opportunity to break away from the traditions and beliefs of his family, his faith and trust in God did not wane. When taken from prison to interpret the dreams of Pharaoh his first words to the king were: It is not in me to interpret the dreams; only God can do so.

Following the interpretation of the two dreams of Pharaoh and rise to power he spends his royal position administrating the country for the benefit of everybody, citizens and foreigners alike. When his brothers came down to Egypt to buy food, he had every reason to avenge the cruelty they had once displaced towards him. How would he treat them? The slave had become a ruler and they were now in his power. Would he take revenge by imprisoning or putting them to death? No. On his brothers showing their remorse for their past behaviour, he takes every care to put them at ease. He says to them: 'I am Joseph whom you sold

46

into Egypt. And now be not grieved, nor angry with yourselves, that you sold me here, for God did send me before you to preserve life' (ibid. v. 7). He then continues to reassure them: 'And God had sent me before you ... to save you alive for a great deliverance' (ibid. v. 7).

What magnanimity! Joseph reassures them that all that happened was part of a divine plan and that his brothers were agents of God. At the end of Parashat Vayechi following the death of the patriarch Jacob, Joseph's brothers were afraid that he would repay them for all the evil that they had done to him. Once again, Joseph assures them: 'Fear not; for am I in the place of God? You meant evil against me, but God meant it for good, to bring to pass, as it is this day, to keep many people alive' (ibid. 50:20).

Let us quote some of our commentators on Joseph's response to his brothers. He said: 'Am I God? I am unable to harm you even if I wished, for the Holy One blessed be He meant it for good' (Rashi). The Sforno explains Joseph's words 'Am I able to judge you, God sent me as an agent of Him.' The Rambam writes: 'Joseph said: "You have not sinned. The Holy One blessed be He caused you to act so for good."'

The Psalmist tells us that 'The righteous deals generously and gives' (37:21). This was Joseph, a righteous Jew who showed us that there was a purpose, a noble purpose, in all that had happened. He stands up as a perfect role model of how one should look at life's events. He is a man unspoilt by good fortune and who sees in prosperity the opportunity of benefiting others. Joseph's life is a glorious example that one needs to remember and follow as a Jew.

13

Vayyechi
JEWISH IDENTITY

And Jacob called unto his sons and said:
'Gather yourselves together, that I may tell you that which
will befall you in the end of days.'

Genesis 49:1

T THE END of the Book of Genesis, we are told that Jacob, before he died, gathered his twelve sons and wished to tell them what would happen at the end of days. Midrash Rabbah explains that Jacob wished to disclose the future but the prophetic vision was concealed from him.

The question one must ask is: What did Jacob wish to disclose? What was the message he wished to convey but was prevented from doing so? One of the answers is that he wished to reveal how the Jewish people were to survive in the Diaspora and Israel until the Messianic era. He wished to divulge how Jews would be able to withstand exile during its recurrence throughout history.

Our Sages inform us that following the passing away of Jacob's children, the physical and spiritual exile began in Egypt. The Torah records in the first chapter of Exodus how the Israelites were becoming too numerous and were considered a threat to the Egyptians. Though initially they entered Egypt as *'gerim'* ('sojourners – temporary residents') in time they secured for themselves a permanent foothold in the land. 'The children of Israel were fruitful, increased and became strong, waxed increasingly and the land was filled with them' Exodus 1:7). Yes, not just in Goshen but everywhere in Egypt they were to be found. As Rashi puts it: 'Even the amphitheatres and circuses were full of them.'

Indeed, many commentators explain that the cause of persecution and bondage was punishment as the Israelites had violated Jacob's wish to live apart from the Egyptians in Goshen. When they sought to integrate with the Egyptian people, God turned the love which the Egyptians bore them into one of hatred (see *Ha'amek Davar*). It was this sin of intermingling and socialising for which they were punished. The objections to any form of assimilation are frequently mentioned in the Torah. Already Joseph, after being reunited with his family, tells Pharaoh that his brothers were shepherds. This was with the intention of preventing them from becoming part of Egyptian society. Even the philosopher and soothsayer Balam recognised Israel's mission to remain separate and distinct from the nations. Prophetically, he recognises this in the words: 'Behold! It is a nation that shall dwell alone and shall not be counted among the nations' (Numbers 23:9). The Gemara in Sanhedrin 104a explains the verse as: 'It is God's will that the Jewish people neither mix nor gain the respect of others for at the end it will lead to loss of our identity as Jews.'

When reading of the bondage and ultimate redemption of the children of Israel, the Torah stresses that gaining their freedom was not an end in itself but a means of entering into a special relationship with God. Moses was told on the commencement of his mission: 'On bringing the people out of Egypt you shall serve God on this mountain (Sinai)' (Exodus 2:12). By accepting the Torah, Am Israel would become a '*goy kadosh*' ('a holy nation') (Exodus 19:6).

In order to preserve the laws and customs of Israel, particularly when it could lead to intermarriage as mentioned in Deuteronomy 7:3 'Neither shall you marry with them; your daughter you shall not give to his son, nor his daughter shall you take for your son', the Rabbis instituted the laws of '*Chukkat Hagoi*', following in the practices of other nations. They therefore ruled we should thus not participate in any wedding festivity of a non-Jew, nor drink their wine nor permit them to touch our wine. They further forbade the consumption of any Jewish dish cooked or baked by a non-Jew unless we assist them in some way (if only by lighting the fire) (Yoreh Deah 112,113).

The dangers of intermarriage and the imperative of avoiding it is stressed on a number of occasions in the Torah. Moses speaks of the evil results of such marriages (Exodus 34:16; Deuteronomy 7/3) and its effects on the nation.

Unfortunately, this danger exists even today. The problem of intermarriage concerns us not just in the Diaspora but in Israel itself. There are over 250,000 immigrants from the former Soviet Union who are not considered halachic Jews, and the Rabbanut in Israel are making every effort within the halachic framework to assist in their conversions. When the question of the Ethiopian aliyah to Israel was raised, the Rishon LeZion, Rabbi Ovadia Yosef, took a courageous step in declaring them to be Jewish.

Let us hope and pray that as we enter Pesach, *zeman cherutenu*, with compassion, vision and understanding, our mission to preserve the unity of our people is paramount in our identity as Jews.

14

Shemot

THREE HEROINES

But the midwives feared God ... and he became her son.

Exodus 1:17; 2:10

MONG the many contributions made by notable figures in the Bible, three are mentioned in today's parasha. They are: Yocheved, Miriam and Bithiah, the daughter of Pharaoh. Each of them played an influential role in the oppression of the Israelites in Egypt.

The Book of Exodus begins with Israel's enslavement and relates that a new king arose who, seeing how numerous the Israelites had become, sought ways to solve the 'Jewish Problem'. Pharaoh and his advisors, not considering it a wise step to kill the Jews publicly, devised ways to destroy them.

The first plan was to prevent their increase by subjecting them to forced labour but when this failed, he proposed the killing of all new-born male babies. Finally, failing in his second plan, Pharaoh ordered his people to drown all male babies born that day.

However, God's providence overruled the evil plans of humans and through the instrument of the three women, brought redemption to the Israelites. The first was Yocheved, wife of Amram, from the tribe of Levi. The second was Miriam, her daughter, and the third was Bithiah, the daughter of Pharaoh.

Yocheved was born during the journey of the Israelites to Egypt and was a hundred and thirty years old when she gave birth to Moses (*Midrash Haggadah Genesis* 23:1).

Yocheved gave birth to Moses after her remarriage to her husband who had divorced her because of Pharaoh's decree that all children born to the Israelites be drowned.

Due to her righteousness, the birth of Moses was a painless one, indicating thereby that she was not included in the punishment of Eve to bear children in pain (*Sotah* 12b).

The second great woman was Miriam, the daughter of Amram and Yocheved. According to tradition she was instrumental in the birth of Moses. The Talmud records that when her father divorced his wife because of Pharaoh's cruel decree, she prophesied that by the re-marriage of her parents a child born would become the redeemer of Israel. Amram listened to her and remarried Yocheved (*Sotah* 12a).

Our Biblical commentators, Rashi for instance, were of the view that the two midwives who saved the new-born babies were Yocheved and Miriam. Quoting the Gemara: 'Rav and Samuel said: "A mother and daughter identifies them to be Yocheved and Miriam."' (ibid.). Thus Shifra is Yocheved, so-called because she ensured the survival of the baby; whilst Puah is Miriam because she talked and pacified the crying infant. These two Jewish midwives, by risking their own lives to save the babies from death (as the Torah records) were blessed with dynasties. Yocheved became the ancestress of Cohanim and Levites, and Miriam became an ancestress of King David.

Tradition has it that Miriam was rewarded to have illustrious descendants including King David because she courageously brought her mother Yocheved to nurse him. In the Talmud it is recorded that due to her courage and resourcefulness like her brothers, Aaron and Moses, she died by a ''Divine Kiss' since the Angel of Death had no power over her' (*Baba* 17a)

Bithiah, Pharaoh's daughter, is the third heroine who was willing to sacrifice her own life to save Moses and raise him as her own child. According to a Midrash, she converted to Judaism and was one of those who entered Paradise in her lifetime (*Rabbah* 18:3).

Our Sages point out that the hatred and jealousy that led Pharaoh to plan the annihilation of children were thwarted by these heroines, who each in her own way played a major role in the birth of Moses, a man destined to become the leader, liberator and greatest prophet in Israel. The greatness of these women is reflected in the Rabbinic statement: 'In the merit of righteous women Israel was redeemed from Egypt' (*Talmud Sotah* 10b).

Indeed, their moral courage and moral responsibility together with the fact that these women feared God foiled the evil plan of Pharaoh. They resisted the command of the king and risked their lives rather than allow so heinous a crime. Moreover, it was because of their love, sacrifice and devotion that our people were enabled to survive and prosper.

These three heroines, like many others in Jewish history, were neither leaders nor held any official positions, yet by their bravery and practical ingenuity they earned a high place in the life of the nation. Indeed, both in Biblical times and up till today, there have been notable women who stand out as an inspiration and bring blessings to our world.

15

Vaera

THE TEN PLAGUES

And I will harden Pharaoh's heart and multiply
My signs and My wonders in the land of Egypt.

Exodus 7:3

And Egypt shall know that I am the Lord.

ibid. v.5

MOSES, at the commencement of his mission to liberate the Israelites from Egyptian servitude, is informed by God that He will bring punishment upon Pharaoh and his people. Isaac Abravanel, the fifteenth century biblical commentator, explains the significance of the ten plagues. He writes that the first three plagues of blood, frogs and gnats came to prove the existence of God as creator of the universe. The next three plagues of swarms of flies, killing of the livestock, and boils taught God's Providence. The last three of hail, locusts and darkness showed that God can change the nature of things at will. Thus the purpose of the plagues was to make Pharaoh and his people aware of God's justice and retribution.

In answer to the question: 'Why did God select just these plagues upon the Egyptians?' the rabbis say the plagues were a punishment, 'measure for measure' ('*midah kneged midah*') (Midrash Rabba 9:9), that the Egyptians were reaping the fruits of their own wicked deeds.

Let us quote the Midrashim on the significance of some of the plagues. The first plague of water transformed into blood was brought about because Pharaoh and the Egyptians worshipped the Nile and threw the children of the Israelites into it. Therefore, God punished the Egyptians by striking it and turning its water into blood. In the ninth plague, the Torah states: 'There was a thick darkness in all the land of Egypt for three days, they saw not one another, neither rose any from his place for three days' (Exodus 10:22, 23). One may ask what is the reason for this thick darkness throughout Egypt where '*lo ra'u ish et achiv*' ('where one saw not his brother'). It was the philosophy of individualism which existed at that time not to be concerned for the welfare of others. Every person lived for himself with little concern for the plight of others. The suffering and the oppression of the Israelites were of no importance to the individual and so '*lo kamu ish mi-tachtov*' ('no man rose out of himself to see his brother'). On the other hand, 'for all the Israelites there was light in the dwellings' (Exodus 10:23).

The Rabbis in the Midrash actually raised this very question: from where did such a thick darkness descend on Egypt? Rabbi Judah said: 'This thick darkness came from above.' Rabbi Nehemiah said: 'The thick darkness came from below. The Gehinna opened its jaws and let loose a part of its own thick darkness.'

These Sages wished to know why thick darkness descended upon such a mighty nation. Rabbi Nehemiah was of the opinion that the darkness came from below; the ordinary members of society were selfish and brutal and saw bondage as part of a national policy. Rabbi Judah, however, considered that the darkness came from above; that those who occupied the higher positions in life – the priests, teachers and philosophers – who had influence and prestige, believed and taught that cruelty and crushing oppression of strangers were the only ideal of life for Egyptians to follow.

Whilst the plagues were brought upon Egypt as a punishment, measure for measure, the ultimate purpose of the plagues was educational, to bestow knowledge of God upon Pharaoh and his people. Pharaoh, when first requested by Moses to set the Israelites free, said: 'Who is the Lord that I must obey Him?... I know not the Lord and moreover I will not let Israel go.' (Exodus 5:2) He finally came to recognise God by declaring: 'The Lord is righteous and I and my people are wicked' (ibid. 9:27).

Let us conclude by quoting a midrash on the disciplinary manner in which the plagues occurred. Our Sages say: 'See how different are the ways of God from the ways of men. When a mighty warrior wishes to destroy his enemy he attacks him in surprise, with the intention of killing him. God, on the other hand, warned Pharaoh ten times, and on each occasion gave him the opportunity to repent in the hope that he would let the Israelites go free.'

16

Bo

THE SPIRITUAL HERITAGE

It is because of this the Lord did for me when I came out of Egypt.
                                                                    Exodus 13:8

ON FOUR occasions, the Torah calls on us to teach our children and guide them in the path of our Jewish faith. Let us enumerate the four passages which our Sages associate with the Haggadah, recited at the Seder table.

These four are: 1. 'When your children say to you: "What is the meaning of this?" you shall say: "It is the sacrifice of the Lord's Passover, when He passed over the house of the children of Israel in Egypt"' (Exodus 12:26, 27).

2. 'And you shall tell your son on that day, saying: "It is because of this the Lord did for me when I came out of Egypt."' (ibid. 13:8)

3. 'And it shall be when your son will ask you at some future time: "What is this?" you shall say to him: "With a strong hand the Lord brought me out of Egypt, from the house of bondage."' (ibid. 13:14)

4. 'When your child in time will ask you: "What means the testimonies, statues and laws which our God commanded you?" you shall say to him: "We were Pharaoh's slaves in Egypt, and the Lord brought us out of Egypt with a mighty hand."' (Deuteronomy 6:20–21).

Telling the story of slavery and of the exodus from Egypt to our children is an essential part of the duty of a parent towards future generations. It stands as a reminder of Jewish identity in which we link the past history of our people to the present and future. It is not just a bond between parents and their offspring but it makes them aware of our roots.

Jewish education transmits our heritage in a manner which the child will understand and according to his intellectual perception. Throughout our history, whilst other nations built pyramids, palaces and castles, we built schools, yeshivot and houses of study. Through the education of the young, though living in ghettos, we were able to create a society in which the young would be taught Torah values of freedom, justice and kindness.

From this tradition of putting education first, the principle emerged which led Rabbinical exposition to the development of the four sons, the wise, the wicked, the simple and the one who needs to be shown the way. The whole purpose of the Haggadah was 'to tell your son' (levincha) which is the central feature of the celebration. This, indeed, explains the development of the Haggadah which took form at the beginning of the second century C.E by 'the Men of the Great Assembly' (*anshei knesset hagedolah*). Its final editing took place at the end of the Talmudic era by the early Geonim, heads of the academies of Sura and Pumpedita. So the narrative is a collection of excerpts from the Bible, Mishna and Midrash. To these were added stories, psalms and songs together with midrashic explanations.

One finds today many recensions of the Haggadah, differing from one another to a greater or lesser degree, which are preserved in various manuscripts, some of which were found in the Cairo Genizah. For all that, the main purpose of the Haggadah was that parents should remain true to the importance of Jewish education in the home. It is the children about whom the Torah speaks in the four texts described earlier. The text 'And you shall tell your son' recalls the ongoing responsibility for the parent to educate his children on the significance of Divine Providence in the redemption of our people from Egypt and throughout history.

But the responsibility to educate one's children was not just a duty confined to the Seder night service. Twice daily, we are told in the Shema: 'And you shall teach them diligently to your children and speak of them when you sit in your house and when you walk by the way, and when you lie down and when you rise up' (Deuteronomy 6:7).

In Gemara Kiddushin, the Mishna states: 'The father is bound to teach his son Torah (29a). Such importance was placed on this command that once Rabbi Hiyya bar Abba saw Rabbi Joshua ben Levi hurriedly taking his child to study. 'What is the reason for this?' he asked. 'The education of my child is very important,' answered Rabbi

Joshua. From that day Rabbi Hiyya did not taste food until he took his child to school (ibid. 30a).

Before the destruction of the Second Temple, if a child had a father, his father taught him, and if he had no father, he did not learn at all. Joshua ben Gamla then ordained a system of education that teachers be appointed in every town and city so that all children, rich or poor, would receive a proper Jewish education. The leaders of his generation praised him: 'May Joshua ben Gamla be always blessed for, but for him, the Torah would have been forgotten from Israel.' However, notwithstanding the role of teachers, there will always remain the duty of a father to educate and train his children in the Jewish way of life and service of God.

17

Beshalach

NOT BY BREAD ALONE

Then the Lord said to Moses: Behold, I will cause bread to rain from heaven for you; and the people shall go out and gather a day's portion, that I may prove them whether they will walk in My law or not.

Exodus 16:4

BOTH in this week's sidra and in Deuteronomy 8:16, the Torah describes the manna as a proof, test or trial for the Jewish people. There we are also told: 'God fed you with the manna in the wilderness ... that He might put you to the test.'

Our biblical commentators are puzzled as to the significance of the test. Normally, a proof or test is something to be borne or a challenge undertaken. Isaac Abravanel, the fifteenth century biblical commentator and philosopher, asks: 'What was the trial by which God provided them daily with bread to eat? On the contrary, far from being a test, did it not constitute an extraordinary example of God's kindness?' He further considers: 'The provision of their daily bread, with a double portion for the Sabbath eve, was an act of great kindness rather than a test. So in what lay the trial?'

Rashi, Rabbi Solomon ben Yitzchak, the eleventh/twelfth century biblical and talmudic commentator, explains that the test was whether they would keep the precepts connected therewith, that they should not leave over the manna for the next day, nor go out to gather on the Sabbath day. Nachmanides, the Ramban, suggests that the manna was a great trial for the children of Israel, for it was given to them in the wilderness without food of any sort except for the manna which melted in the heat of the sun. This daily rationing was to prove the extent of faith and trust in their Creator. A similar comment is made by the Rashbam, a grandson of Rashi. He explains the trial not in terms of suffering but in their dependence 'that I may prove him – since every day they would rely for their sustenance upon God'. The trial was then to demonstrate whether they would have absolute faith or not and remain in total dependence on the Almighty.

Playing on the words: 'A day's portion every day', Rabbi Eliezer the Modaite said: 'Whosoever has the necessary means or resources for today and says 'What shall I eat tomorrow?' shows a lack of faith, as it is stated: 'that I may prove him whether he will walk in My law' (Mekhilta; T. Sotah 48b). From the above, we see that the test of the manna was to prove absolute reliance on God for their daily sustenance, one of faith and obedience.

Reverting to one of the verses in Deuteronomy which we stated before is the phrase 'Man does not live by bread alone, but by everything that proceeds out of the mouth of the Lord does man live' (8:3). What, we may ask, is the meaning of this text? The next question would then be 'What, then, does man live by?' The Torah answers both these questions by informing us. We live 'by everything that proceeds out of the mouth of the Lord'. But we still do not know what the Bible means by this.

Rabbi Samson Raphael Hirsch offers us an insight into the meaning of our text. He writes: 'The manna daily given to the Israelites in the desert wanted them to learn the wonderful goodness of God and to teach that even in the midst of poverty and hardship life is sustained by Divine love.' (Horeb 11:78,83). It was through privations and suffering during those forty years that they were to learn the power of God who sustains all life.

Furthermore, man, we know, consists of a body and a soul. Judaism teaches that in order to be healthy, one needs to provide for the welfare of both. Unlike some other beliefs, Judaism is opposed to a life of asceticism where we are called upon to withdraw from the legitimate pleasures of the world. Yet, whilst not denying the importance of satisfying our bodily needs we need also to think of our spiritual nature. Physical nourishment is not the only thing that ensures our existence. The Torah teaches us that man has a soul as well as a body and that it is not by bread alone that we live but by the spiritual life, the teachings contained in the Torah – 'by everything that proceeds out of the mouth of the Lord does man live'. It is indeed by the teachings proclaimed to us on Mount Sinai that we Jews continue to live and thrive.

18

Yitro

PARENTS AND CHILDREN

*Honour your father and your mother that your days may be long
upon the land which the Lord your God has given you.*

Exodus 20:12

*Hear my son, the instruction of your father and
forsake not the teaching of your mother.*

Proverbs 1:8

AT THE FOOT of Mount Sinai, the Jewish people received its natural
character. Up to that time they had become free from Egyptian
slavery but, with the acceptance of God's covenant, they became
a holy nation, an '*am segulah*' (a precious treasure) unto God.

In the fifth of the Ten Commandments, the Torah commands us to
honour our parents. This law, engraved on the first tablet, was
addressed to every individual man and woman and applied both during
their life and after their death. The obligation to respect one's parents is
taught in the following Gemara: 'The Torah says: "Honour your father
and your mother" (Exodus 20:12) and it also says "Honour God with
your property"' (Proverbs 3:9). By using the same language in both
instances, scripture puts the honour due to one's parents on the same
level as the honour due to the Omnipresent. Furthermore, the Rabbis
taught 'There are three partners in the creation of a person: The Holy
One, blessed be He, his father and his mother. Whenever a person
honours his father and mother, it is considered as if I have been
honoured' (Kiddushim 30b).

This filial duty to respect and honour one's parents is a duty not to
be taken lightly. It involves time, physical effort and financial sacrifice
as well as consideration and understanding. The following story
illustrates the importance of this command. The mother of Rabbi Tarfon

61

once came out of her home on the Shabbat to walk in her garden when the buckle of her shoe broke. Rabbi Tarfon, who was with her, stooped and placed his hands under her feet and slowly helped her back to her home (Yerushalmi Peah 1).The Sages relate that the Nasi Rabbi Simeon ben Gamliel would say that although he served and attended to his father all his lifetime, he did not honour him to the extent of even one hundredth part of the extent to which Esau honoured his father. He explained: 'When I attended to my father I wore ordinary clothes. Esau, however, always attended to his father in his best clothes' (Midrash Bereshit Rabbah 61).

The Talmud relates how a non-Jew, Darma ben Natina, showed extraordinary affection and respect towards his parent. On one occasion, his father had in his possession a precious stone which was needed for the High Priest's breastplate. The Rabbis offered the son an enormous sum of six hundred thousand golden dinars but, at the time, Darma's father was asleep and the key of the safe where the stone was lodged lay under his head. Darma refused to sell them the jewel as he wished not to awaken his father. On another occasion, Darma's mother, who was insane, saw him dressed in silk and gold. She struck him in the face with a shoe, tore his garments and spat on his face, yet he did not shame her (Kiddushin 31).

The honour to one's parents is so important that Judah ibn Tibbon, an outstanding scholar and physician of the twelfth century, reminds his son in his ethical will of his devotion in raising him up. His letter reads: 'You should know, my son, how I brought you up and how I led you in the paths of wisdom and virtue. I fed and clothed you: I spent my time educating and protecting you. I sacrificed my sleep to make you wise and to raise you to the highest degree of science and morals. These years I have denied myself the usual pleasures and relaxations of men for your sake and I still toil for your future' (Kobler, *Letters of Jews through the Ages*, p. 157).

Let us conclude by stating that there is nothing more beautiful or more valuable than love and respect for one's parents. The fundamental filial feeling of honour and respect for the fifth commandment does not apply merely to attending to the physical and financial needs of those who brought us into the world. It should, at all times, be prompted by the sincere gratitude and thankfulness demanded by the Torah.

19

Mishpatim
THE HEBREW SLAVE

If you buy a Hebrew servant, six years he shall serve; and in the seventh year he shall go out free without paying for his release.

Exodus 21:2

And if a man sells his daughter to be a maid-servant, she shall not go out as the men servants do.

ibid. 7

A FUNDAMENTAL principle of Judaism is the sacredness of human personality. Every person is the property of God and therefore cannot become the property or chattel of another. In ancient times, Hebrew slavery was commonly accepted but was quite different from Greek or Roman slavery. In Jewish law, the slave did not belong to the master nor was he to be treated in an undignified manner. Any brutal treatment by the master would liberate the slave, whether he was a Hebrew or non-Jew.

Philo, a Jewish philosopher of the first century, gives us an insight into ancient Roman law where the head of a family was considered the master and had unlimited authority. He writes: 'Parents have not only been given the rights of exercising authority over their children ... but had their legal status enforced by law' (Vol. 7 of his writings 'On The Special Laws' 2:23).

In Jewish law, however, parents – particularly fathers – had legal rights over their children while they were minors, but even such authority was limited. Once children reached majority, the age of thirteen years and one day for a boy and twelve years and six months for a girl, they had no further legal authority over them. The legal rights which the father had over his daughter as expressed in the Bible or understood by the Rabbis were three in number. He could take a husband for his daughter, he could sell her as a Hebrew maid-servant and he could annul her vow.

When it came to marriage, the father had the right to betroth his daughter as long as she was a '*ketanah*' (i.e. under the age of twelve years) or until she showed signs of puberty or while a '*naarah*' (i.e. during the six months period between the age of twelve and twelve years and six months). When it came to selling her as a maid-servant, he could do so as long as she was a '*ketanah*', a minor. As to annulling her vows, his authority was limited to the period when she was a '*naarah*' and not a minor (Sifre, Numbers, 153). If a father sold his daughter while she was a minor she had to be set free as soon as she showed signs of puberty. One who acquired a minor as a maid-servant was obliged to take her for a wife for himself or for his son. According to our Sages, a father could sell his minor daughter as a maid-servant on the understanding that her master or his son would marry her.

Hebrew slaves, whether male or female, were not in Jewish law considered slaves in the usual accepted sense. Commenting on the text: 'If you buy a Hebrew servant, six years he shall serve' (Exodus 21:2) the Mekhilta explains this: 'One might understand this to mean any kind of service, but it is said: "You shall not make him to serve as a bondservant" (Leviticus 25:39). So a Hebrew slave must not wash the feet of his master, nor put his shoes on him, nor carry his things when going to the bathhouse, nor carry him on a stretcher or chair as other slaves do. He should not be doing any work which humiliates him nor be put to work forcibly in anything other than his trade. Furthermore, he works only during the day and not during the night.'

We see from this passage that, by Jewish law, slaves were not the property of their masters and that the latter had no ownership over them. The Gemara in Kiddushin elaborates further on the rights of the Hebrew slave. The Torah defines: 'Because it will be good with you' (Deuteronomy 15:16) to mean 'you should not eat white bread and he black bread; you should not drink old wine and he new wine; you should not sleep on feathers and he on straw' (20a).

Maimonides, in his Guide for the Perplexed, speaking of Jewish slavery, shows that while slavery was permitted in ancient times the laws relating to them are all 'mercy, compassion and forbearance'. He continues: 'You are duty bound to see that your slave makes progress; you must benefit him and not hurt him ... and when fortune is good to you, do not deny him his portion' (3:39).

20

Terumah
PRAISE AND THANKSGIVING

Then sang Moses and the children of Israel this song unto the Lord.

Exodus 15:1

Then sang Deborah and Barak the son of Avinoam on that day.

Judges 5:1

And David spoke unto the Lord the words of this song.

Samuel II 22:1

The song of all songs dedicated to God,
Him to whom peace belongs.

Song of Songs 1:1

SONGS of praise and thanksgiving to God mentioned in the Torah are expressions of gratitude to the Holy One, blessed be He, for His goodness to the House of Israel. The first song mentioned in the Bible is that of the deliverance at the Red Sea from the hand of Pharaoh and his pursuing army. So unique was this experience of divine intervention that our Sages, commenting on the verse: 'This is my God and I will glorify Him' (Exodus 15:2), say that even a maidservant at the Red Sea saw vividly more than many a Prophet (Rashi quoting the Mekhilta).

The songs of praise for deliverance from our enemies by Deborah and King David also tell of divine intervention which saved Israel from its oppressors. In these songs of thanksgiving both Deborah and David trace Providence for their victories from threatened calamity.

When one comes to Shir HaShirim (Song of Songs) composed by King Solomon, our Sages say: 'It is the greatest of all songs uttered to the Holy One, blessed be He' (Rashi). Written in the form of an allegory, it is a passionate dialogue between the husband (God) who loves the Jewish people and his wife (Israel). Despite its brevity (it consists of nine chapters) Rabbi Akiva commented: 'The entire world only existed for the day on which the Song of Songs was given to Israel.' He further declared: 'All the writings in the Torah are holy, but this song is the most holy ' (Mishna Yadayim 3:5). Once again, he further stated: 'He who chants the Song of Songs as a secular song forfeits his share in the world to come' (Tosefta Sanhedrin 12).

Tradition has it that King Solomon foresaw through the Holy Spirit – (*Ruach Hakodesh*) – that Israel is destined to suffer a series of exiles, and will lament, recalling her former status as God's chosen beloved. She will say: 'I shall return to my first husband (God) for it was better then than now' (Hosea 2:9). It was this relationship between God and Israel who has strayed and seeks to endure herself to Him once more, as she recalls her youthful love for Him. God, too, is 'afflicted by her afflictions '(Isaiah 63:9) and proclaims that she is not cast away permanently. She still remains His wife and He her husband and will yet return to her.

Rabbi Yossi quoting the Zohar said: 'King Solomon was inspired to compose this Song when the Holy Temple was built as a replica of the Holy Temple above. On that day, there was no greater joy before the Holy One, from the day the world was created.'

The Targum (the translation of the Bible into Aramaic – see Talmud Megilla 3a) explains that only ten songs were composed to God, and Solomon's Song of Songs is elevated above all.

The Psalmist says that all of creation praises and tells of the glory of God. To the Rabbis, as reflected in an esoteric but little book called '*Perek Shira*' (Chapter of Song) every part of creation, from the sun to the ant, from the bird to the frog, sings its only song of praise to God. But it is for man – the noblest of all creation – to perceive the glory and greatness of God and to acknowledge this through praise.

Rambam, speaking on man's creation and mission in life, writes: 'When a person meditates upon God's wondrous and good deeds and sees His infinite wisdom, immediately he loves, praises, exalts and feels a great urge to express this through song' (Yesodei Hatorah 2:2). This, indeed, should be one's purpose in life: to see the Divine Presence at all times and express it through song and praise.

Solomon ibn Gabirol, the distinguished author and philosopher of the Golden Age of Spain, in his poem 'The Royal Crown' 'Keter Malchut' calls upon the human mind to reflect and admire God's greatness in his creation of the universe. In his introduction he writes: 'Wonderful, O God, are your works; and this my soul knows fully well. Thine, O Lord, is the greatness, power, glory, victory and majesty. Thine, O Lord, is the kingdom. You are praised and exalted as Supreme above all. Who can describe your greatness... who can recount the praises due to You'.

21

Tetzaveh

MAKE ME A SANCTUARY

And let them make for Me a Sanctuary,
that I may dwell among them.

Exodus 25:8

And I will dwell among the children of Israel,
and will be their God.

Exodus 29:45

THE COMMAND to the children of Israel in the wilderness to build a Tabernacle was given with the object of spiritualising their lives. Long before they settled in Eretz Yisrael, there was a need for a spiritual centre which would unite them as one people. That centre was to be a 'sanctuary' (*mikdash*) where God's glory would abide.

One of the questions that our commentators ask is: What lay behind the command to build this portable Tabernacle? According to the Midrash, Moses was commanded to do so after the people worshipped the golden calf. 'On the Day of Atonement the sin for the golden calf was forgiven and on that same day the Holy One, blessed be He, said to Moses: 'Let them make me a sanctuary that I may dwell among them, so that all the nations should know that I have forgiven them' (Tanchuma). Rashi maintains this view: that the story of the golden calf took place before the command to build the Tabernacle and that it was after their reconciliation with God. Thus, the object of the Tabernacle in the midst of the people was in order to spiritualise their lives as well as to be a '*mishkan ha'edut*' (a tabernacle of testimony) to the whole world, that God was reconciled with Israel after their grievous sin.

The question one may then ask is: How can we reconcile the physical construction of a building with God's infinity? Did not the prophet Isaiah say of Him: 'The heaven is My throne and the earth My footstool – where is the house that you may build for Me and where the place of My rest?' (66:1). Similarly, King Solomon said in building the Temple: 'Behold, the heaven, and heaven of heavens cannot contain Thee, how much less this house that I have built?' (Kings I, 8:27).

Isaac Abravanel answers this by saying that the construction of the Tabernacle was to combat the belief that God, after creating it, had forsaken the earth. To deny such a view He commanded them to make this edifice, believing that God lived in their midst and that His Providence was ever with them.

Rashi, in his commentary, explains the text: 'They shall make for Me a Sanctuary.' This building was to be a structure dedicated to God's service, that is, a place from which the nation would be spiritually uplifted and receive inspiration.

This is how the Sefer Hachinuch formulates the precept of erecting a central place of worship: 'The underlying purpose of this command is for no other reason but to promote our well-being. He showed us the way of right conduct ... The building of a house in His name for us to perform therein acts of prayer and sacrifice was inspired by our needs, to put us in the right frame to worship Him ... That is why He commanded us to set aside a place of the highest purity, there to purify the thoughts of man and refine his character.'

A similar idea is expressed by Hertz in the words 'that I may dwell among them' – that the sanctuary was the symbol of holiness which was to be the rule of life for the Israelites ... They were to hold themselves aloof from everything that was defiling, because God was amongst them.'

The Malbim offers another reason for the command. 'He commanded that each individual should build a sanctuary in the recesses of his heart and prepare himself to be a dwelling place for the Lord's presence.' Thus, the Sanctuary was not the sole dwelling place of God but a symbol of that holiness which was to be the rule of conduct for Israel.

From the above commentaries, one understands the deep significance and importance that the Tabernacle played in spiritualising the lives of Israel and unifying them as one people.

22

Ki Tissa

ACCOUNTABILITY

When you take the sum of the children of Israel, according to their number
... this they shall give, everyone that passes among them that are
numbered, half a shekel ... for an offering to the Lord.

Exodus 30:12–13

THE PARSHAH commences with the mitzvah of 'the half-shekel' (*machatzit hashekel*) which every adult Jew was required to give when he was about to go into battle. Besides this primary purpose, the half-shekel was used for the bases of the pillars of the Tabernacle as well as for the hooks to keep the boards together (see Exodus 38:27). Later on, the half-shekel tax was collected annually in the month of Adar to maintain the use of sacrifices in the Temple whereby the whole House of Israel shared in this daily act of public worship.

The giving of the half-shekel, where the rich were not to give more, nor the poor less, conveyed a message that in the eyes of God we are all equal. It further taught that though only a half-shekel was to be paid, an insignificant sum, it was an important symbol of the individual's attachment to the nation. By equal participation, all Jews shared in the unity of a nation working together towards a common goal. This concept of unity is expressed in Pirke Avot: 'All who work for the community should do so for the sake of Heaven ... For (God will say) I count you worthy of great reward as though you yourselves had accomplished it all' (2:2).

We thus see the great power of a people when everyone joins together. It is this contribution that helps towards the fulfilment of any complete work and the law of a half-shekel emphasised the responsibility of the individual to the community as well as the interdependence between man and his fellow man.

The appointment of those who hold the finance of the community was of concern to our Sages. The Torah explicitly states the principle: 'And you shall be guiltless before the Lord and before Israel' (Numbers 32:22). The public always suspect the intentions of those who hold office and every effort must be made by a public servant to be above suspicion. The following Midrash dwells on this. Commenting on the text: 'These are the accounts of the Tabernacle, even the Tabernacle of the testimony, as they were rendered according to the commandment of Moses' (Exodus 38:21). The Rabbis ask: Why did Moses render an account of the Tabernacle? Surely the Holy One, blessed be He, trusted him, as it says: 'He is trusted in all My house' (Numbers 12:7). Notwithstanding, Moses did this. Because the scorners at the time gossiped about him, as it is stated: 'When Moses left the Tent, all the people rose up, and stood, every man at his tent door, and looked at Moses' (Exodus 33:8). Why? 'They looked at his back and said one to another: What a neck! What legs! He eats of that which is ours, and drinks of that which is ours! Fool! replies his fellow. One who is in charge of the work of the Tabernacle, talents of silver, talents of gold, what do you expect that he should not be rich? Moses, when he heard this, said: "As soon as the work is finished I will render them an account." When the Tabernacle was completed, Moses said to them: "These are the accounts of the Tabernacle."' (Tanchuma Pekudei).

From this we learn that it is not enough for a person to justify his behaviour to God, but he must do the same before Israel. One finds in the Talmud many other examples in which people who held public office sought to keep themselves above suspicion (see Gemara Yoma 38a and Shekalim 3:2) and strove to be pure before God and Israel. Here are two. The house of Garmu were experts in the making of the showbread, but never was fine bread found in the hands of their children lest people would say: 'They grow fat from the preparation of the showbread.' (Yoma 38a).

The person who went up to take an offering from the shekel-chamber did not wear a sleeved coat or shoes or sandals ... lest if he became rich they would say that he became rich from the offerings taken out of the shekel-chamber; for a man must satisfy people even as he must satisfy God (Shekalim 3:2).

From the above our Sages teach us that when we are dealing with public funds, every effort must be made to be above suspicion. Though Moses was honest and trusted by God as it says 'He is trusted in all My house' (Numbers 12:7), yet on the completion of the Tabernacle he said to the nation: 'These are the accounts of the Tabernacle' (Exodus 38:21). Indeed it is important to find grace and favour in the eyes of God and man.

23

Vayyakhel-Pekudei

ONE NATION

*Thus was finished all the work of the Tabernacle of the Tent of Meeting,
and the children of Israel did according to all that the Lord commanded
Moses, so did they do.*

Exodus 39:32

THE CONCLUDING chapters of the Book of Exodus deal with a
detailed description of the construction of the Sanctuary and its
furniture. As explained in Parashat Terumah, the whole of Bnei
Yisrael were called upon to participate in this holy work. But many of
our commentators ask the question: Did all of the Bnei Yisrael
contribute to the making of the Sanctuary? Did the Bnei Yisrael make
it? Was it not done by Bezalel and his wise-hearted craftsmen?

Isaac Abravanel, the fifteenth century philosopher and Biblical
exegete, explains that by including the act of giving the materials, the
Israelites as a whole had played their part in the construction of the
Tabernacle.

The Or Ha-hayim, a Moroccan Talmudist of the seventeenth
century, explains in his commentary that the Torah was given to be
collectively observed by the nation as a whole and that an individual's
donation would benefit every Jew.

Let us quote his words: 'The Almighty gave us 613 precepts and it
is impossible for one person to observe them all. There are, for
example, Priests, Levites, and Israelites, men and women. Some
precepts apply only to priests, others can be only fulfilled by Israelites
and others only by women. In what way is it possible for the individuals
to observe all the precepts, the 248 positive and 365 negative,
corresponding to the limbs and sinews of the human body? The answer
must be that the Torah can be observed collectively, by the people as a
whole, each individual deriving benefit from the observance of his

neighbour and each individual's performance complementing that of the other.'

In dealing with the construction of the Mishkan, there is yet further significance as to the free-will offerings of the entire nation. Standing in the midst of the Israelites, it served as a symbol of the oneness of Israel. The lesson it taught, the idea it conveyed, was that although divided into families and tribes, Israel was one people, united by one common faith and the worship of one God. It served as a symbol and reminder that the Jewish people must always remain a united nation, bound together by the lofty teachings and principles on which Judaism stands.

Indeed the building of the Mishkan stood as a constant reminder that Israel's oneness must at all times be preserved. Just as it had been when all the individual items were brought together and combined as a whole, so also Israel becomes one by the unity of all classes of Jews. It is by standing together as one nation that the Tabernacle served as a symbol of the oneness of Israel. Indeed, our Sages, in speaking of social solidarity and the unity of the Jewish people, said that every Jew should consider himself as a limb of the nation and never exclude himself from it (T.B. Berachot 49b). Indeed, the Jewish people is one indivisible unit and this is the message that the construction of the Mishkan conveyed to us for all times and ages.

When the Tabernacle ceased to exist, the First and Second Temples stood as a spiritual force unifying the Jewish people as one whole. When the two Temples were destroyed, their place was taken by the Synagogue, a 'Mikdesh Meat' a 'Smaller Sanctuary' which exercised a unifying influence upon the nation.

The Synagogue, as a place of communal prayer, is believed to have existed around the sixth century before the common era when the Jews in Babylon and other parts of the Diaspora were separated from their homeland. During the Second Temple it has been estimated there existed hundreds of Synagogues before it was destroyed in the year 70. The Jerusalem Megillah (65:a) records the magnificent Synagogue in Alexandria, Egypt, built in the form of basilica where people of different crafts each had their own appointed places.

Throughout our long and chequered history, the Synagogue as a spiritual home served as a house of prayer, study and communal activities. Although a minority amongst the nations, it has enabled us to overcome all types of dangers. It has been said that there has been no human institution other than the Synagogue which has played a prominent role in unifying us as one people. this remains till today as the Centre, a true small sanctuary, making us one nation where every Jew can find solace in his many troubles.

24

Vayyikra
THE HEART OF MAN

When any man of you brings an offering to the Lord ...
he shall bring it to the door of the tent of meeting,
that he may be accepted before the Lord.

Leviticus 1:2, 3

WE BEGIN the third book of the Torah with the laws of sacrifices. In ancient times, animal sacrifice was common among idolators but as pointed out by Maimonides in his Guide for the Perplexed it was raised to a purely spiritual level in service to one God.

The condition of all the sacrifices was that it be acceptable and pleasing to God. But what were the conditions necessary for an offering to be favourably received by God? Here are some of the views of our Sages on this question. Ibn Ezra explains that the offering was to be done willingly and not under duress. Onkelos is of the opinion that the offering was to be given in the right spirit, emanating from the heart.

It is necessary to point out that with each of the sacrifices, be it the burnt offering, a meal offering, a peace offering or a sin offering, it should be *'re'ach meoach lashem'* – 'a sweet savour to the Lord'. The Talmud, commenting on this expression, states: *'Echad hamarbeh ve'echad hamameet uvilvad she'yechayvin libo leshamayim'* – 'whether he can give much or little it is acceptable so long as the worshipper lifts up his heart to heaven' (Berachot 5b).

The purpose of a sacrifice was to bring about a change in man. No sacrifice, however great, was of value if it did not come from the heart and a desire for improvement. Indeed, God looks at the spirit in which the offering is made: 'For the Lord sees not as man sees, for man looks on the outward appearance, but the Lord looks to the heart.'

Because God looks into the heart of man and judges not by appearances, He regards a good thought as an actual pious act. In Gemara Kiddushin we are told: 'If a person wished to perform a good deed but was prevented from performing it, it is considered as if he had performed it' (40a). From this we learn that what God demands of us is the sincere desire to do good: whether we are able to accomplish it matters not. Furthermore, it says: '*Echad hamarbeh ve'echad hamameet uvilvad she'yechayvin libo leshamayim*' – 'Whether we are able to do much or little is of little importance so long as one directs one's heart towards heaven' (Berachot 5b), since it is the heart that determines the true value of a person's feelings. One must therefore concentrate all our endeavours upon the purification of the heart, to keep it pure from pride and arrogance.

There is an interesting message recorded by our Sages. The Gemara in Kiddushin states: 'A good thought is regarded as a good deed.' Rav Assi said 'Even if a person contemplated fulfilling a mitzvah and was unavoidably prevented from performing it, scripture credits him as if he had fulfilled it' (40:a). From this we learn that a persons desire to do good is important even though at times he may not be able to accomplish it.

Since the Almighty alone sees the heart of man, one should always be careful of judging others by appearances. We all know that appearances can be deceptive, for the human eye can only see that which is on the outside. We know that even the prophet Samuel, in appointing a new king from the house of Jesse, was deceived by the outward appearance, not realising that David, the youngest child, was worthy to be anointed king of Israel. God, however, saw that the heart of David was pure and full of goodness and was therefore fit to be God's anointed. In the Book of Deuteronomy, dealing with a city tainted with idolatry, we are told that if some of their members are accused of serving other gods, then those in authority were 'to inquire and make search and ask diligently if it is true' (13:15). Therefore the law is: '*Vedarashta vehakarta vesha'alta heitev*' – 'You should inquire, and make search, and ask diligently.' Indeed, careful investigation had to be made before any action was taken. Maimonides therefore ruled: 'It is unlawful for one to pass judgement on mere speculation.'

The lesson one takes from the parsha is that God alone sees the heart of man and it is therefore our duty to concentrate all our endeavours upon the purification of the heart and the desire to do good. Yes, *'rachmana liba baee'* – 'the Merciful desires the heart of man'.

25

Tzav

THE SAVING OF HUMAN LIFE

*Then Mordecai said to Esther: 'If you persist in keeping silence at a time
like this, relief and deliverance will come to the Jews from another place ...
And who knows whether it was such a time
as this that you attained the royal position?'*

Esther 4: 13, 14

THE BOOK OF ESTHER relates the story of Esther, an orphaned
cousin of Mordecai, whom Ahasuerus, king of the Persian
Empire, struck by her beauty, made his queen. Haman, a
descendant of Amalek, on being promoted in the royal court, desired to
destroy the Jews, young and old alike. On learning of this Mordecai
approached Esther to save her people, and she risked her life to achieve
their deliverance.

On the second day of the banquet, which she prepared for the king
and Haman, she petitioned: 'If it pleases the king, let my life be granted
to me as my request and my people as my petition. For we have been
sold, I and my people, to be destroyed, slain and exterminated' (ibid.
7:4). On hearing this, the king, in his anger, ordered that Haman be
hanged, and he issued a decree permitting the Jews to gather and defend
themselves on the day that had been set aside for their extermination
(ibid. 8:11).

Although the name of God does not appear in the entire Book of
Esther and the divine countenance is concealed, His presence was there
guiding history and the destiny of the Jewish people. The greatness of
Mordecai and Esther lay in their awareness that at times God's will
might be carried out through the hand of His agents. This was the
challenge that faced them and Mordecai recognised Esther's role as
instrumental in the nation's salvation. It was this message he conveyed
to her: 'And who knows whether it was just for such a time as this that

you attained the royal position' (4:14). Centuries earlier, this message of Divine redemption through human intervention was brought home in the story of Moses' role as liberator of the Jews.

The prophet Moses, when first called upon to be the redeemer of the Israelites from Egyptian slavery, say our Sages, was perplexed that he should be chosen as the instrument of divine providence. He asked of God: 'Who am I that I should go to Pharaoh, and that I should bring forth the children of Israel from Egypt?' (Exodus 3:11). He continued: 'Did you not promise Jacob, when going down to Egypt, "I will bring you up again?" And now You send me to deliver them?' God urged him not to fear Pharaoh because 'I will be with you.' By this Moses was taught the great lesson: 'For I shall be with you' was a message to him and future generations that everything done by humans is part of a divine plan – that God works through agents and that we ourselves can be those agents. Indeed, everyone can be an instrument in carrying out the mission to redeem others from bondage to freedom.

The duty of saving a life is the subject of a special command in the Torah and to the Sages the individual soul is as precious and important as the world itself. The Mishnah in Sanhedrin states: 'The first man was created single – to teach that anyone who destroys a single life is considered by scripture as if he had destroyed an entire world; and whoever preserves a single life is considered by scripture as if he had preserved an entire world.' (37a).

The duty of saving human life can be seen in the following Rabbinic exposition. Commenting on the text: 'You shall not stand idly by the blood of your neighbour: I am the Lord' (Leviticus 19:16) we are told: 'When one sees one's fellow man drowning in a river, or being attacked by a wild beast or thieves, one is obliged to rescue him. Similarly, one must do everything possible to save one's fellow man from one wishing to kill another. If one omits to do so he is guilty of the prohibition of rescuing one's brother' (Midrash Yalkut Shimoni, number 613, Choshen Mishpat 42b). Rabbi Hirsch further comments on this command to rescue one's fellow man from danger. He writes: 'One's mission of preserving one soul is not confined to the precincts of your home or members of your household. Wherever you have power and opportunity to contribute to the welfare of others, do not fail to do so ... Where the life of your neighbour is in danger and you are able by some personal effort or by means of money to obviate the danger and omit to do so, then you transgress this prohibition with which God has placed the rescue of your brother in your hand.' (Horev Section 557)

The story of Purim, celebrated on the fourteenth of Adar, is thus an annual reminder to us of a miracle brought about by a string of events of human intervention that led to our salvation. The redemption of our people by God, through His agents Mordecai and Esther, is a constant reminder to us that, though concealed, He is the source of every occurrence in our lives and rules the affairs of men. This is the message of Purim. God, though unseen by His wise design, averted the changes which threatened Israel's existence by the hands of his righteous ones.

26

Shemini

SANCTIFICATION OF THE BODY

*These are the living things which you may eat among
all the beasts that are on the earth.*

Leviticus 11:2

*I am the Lord your God; sanctify yourselves therefore and be you holy; for
I am holy; neither shall you defile yourselves.*

ibid. 11:44

FOLLOWING the appointment and consecration of Aaron and his sons into the priesthood, the Torah describes the laws relating to clean and unclean animals and the demand for sanctification of the nation. Kashrut, the observance of the dietary laws, has always been one of the fundamentals of Judaism and has enabled our people to survive throughout the ages in the midst of hostile surroundings.

But what really is the object of these dietary laws? The Rabbis state that 'the object of these commandments to Israel is to purify their lives' (Midrash Samuel 4). Through the observance of these laws, the Jew was to learn to discipline himself, and to know which animals, birds and fish may be eaten, and the way in which they were prepared for consumption.

Yehezkel Kaufman, in his History of the Israelite Religion, writes: 'The entire Jewish people is commanded to be holy and to be aware of uncleanness in order to be "a kingdom of priests and a holy nation"' (Book 2, p. 455).

The Sages of the Talmud did not attempt to find rational explanations for the dietary laws. They said: 'For what does the Holy One, Blessed be He, care whether a person kills an animal by the throat or by the nape of the neck; but its purpose is to refine us?' (Genesis Rabbah 44:1, Leviticus Rabbah 13:3). The Rabbis however, maintained that the food one eats does not affect only the body but also the soul, clogging the heart and dulling man's finer qualities. Thus Isaac Arama, a fifteenth century Spanish commentator, states: 'The reason behind all the dietary prohibitions is that they harm the body and the soul, as well as blunt the intellectual powers' (Akedat Yitzchak, Parshat Shemini).

Here is Maimonides' observation as a physician on this subject. 'The food forbidden by the Torah is unwholesome ... The principle reason why the Torah forbids us swine's flesh is to be found in the circumstances that its habits and food are very dirty and loathsome. Our teachers declared: "The mouth of a swine is as filthy as dung itself"' (Guide for the Perplexed 3:48).

Samson Raphael Hirsch maintains that the human body is the medium that connects the outside world with the mind of man. 'Anything which gives the body too much independence, or makes it too active in a carnal direction, brings it to the animal sphere, robbing it of its primary functions, to be the intermediary between the soul of man and the world outside.' (Commentary on Parshat Shemini)

Such a view is also shared by Abravanel. 'The Divine Law comes to protect our spiritual health. It therefore forbids food which revolt the pure and intellectual soul, clogging the human temperament and driving out the pure and holy spirit about which King David exclaimed: "The holy spirit take not from me!"' This precautionary measure also applies to the text: 'Of their flesh you shall not eat, and their carcasses you shall not touch; they are unclean to you' (Leviticus 11:8). Abravanel explains why an animal that has died of unnatural causes is not permitted to us, even if it is kosher, whilst an animal killed by shechitah is: 'That killed by shechitah was healthy and could have survived if it had not been slaughtered; an animal that died of unnatural causes may have died of an infectious disease and its meat may carry the infection into the human body.'

A former Chief Rabbi, J. H. Hertz, makes a further point on the object of the dietary laws. 'They have proved an important factor in the preservation of the Jewish race in the past, and are, in more than one respect, an irreplaceable agency for maintaining Jewish identity in the present' (Pentateuch, p. 448).

We thus see, from the above opinions of our teachers, that these laws of purity on food not only made us a people apart from all others but enabled us to avoid eating creatures that were unwholesome or repulsive or harmful to us.

27

Tazria – Metzora
DIVINE PROVIDENCE

When there appears on a man's skin a swelling, or a scab, or a shiny spot and it develops into a case of leprosy, then he shall be brought to Aaron the priest, or to one of his sons, the priests.

Leviticus 13:2

THE TWO PARSHIOT Thazria – Metzora deal with the laws of leprosy and the purification of the sufferer on his being restored to normal health. According to the Sforno and other commentators, the leprosy which affected the individual was not caused by an infection but was spiritual in nature and a manifestation of a disease of the soul.

The Sages homiletically interpret the word '*metzora*' as connected with '*motzi shem ra*', a person guilty of slander or libel as a divine punishment for this evil (Gemara Arachin 15a).

The power of speech is that which distinguishes a human being from the animal world and he who commits this sin is considered a triple murderer: for he sins against himself, the person who hears it, and the victim. The Bible states that such a person was to be isolated and compelled to dwell outside the Israelite camp until he heals himself through repentance and good deeds.

The Psalmist stresses the importance of not speaking ill of others. 'Who is the man that desires life, who loves days of seeing good? Guard your tongue from evil, and your lips from speaking deceit' (34: 13, 14). He thus reminds us of the power of speech, and if careful, we can be assured that our life on earth will be blessed.

Rabbi Samson Raphael Hirsch dealing with the subject '*Lashon HaRa*' (Listening to Evil) writes: 'One should not listen to malicious talk, which tells you something derogatory about your brother or sister ... For if you listen to him and take in what he says, then you make yourself a partner in his crime, and incur even greater guilt. For if men pledged themselves not to listen to any evil talk, the evil speakers would cease of themselves. However, by listening to evil talk you make tale bearing possible ... and complete the crime of the calumniator, for you bring to ripeness the seed of hatred which he tried to sow' (Horev Section 134).

Belief in Divine Providence, '*Hasgachah Pratit*', is a basic tenet of Judaism. It signifies God's control and the providence of the universe and of the individual. The Gemara in Chullin says: 'A man does not even strike a finger unless it is decreed on high' (7b). A similar thought is expressed in the following Midrash. 'A snake never bites, a lion never rends a government, never interferes unless it is so ordained from above' (Ecclesiastes Rabbah 10:11, 1).

Again, it is related: 'There was a man who sat and expounded: "You will not find a single hair in the body for which the Holy One, blessed be he, has not created a separate perforation in the skin in order that one hair should not benefit from another"' (Leviticus Rabbah 15:3).

Bachya ben Joseph ibn Paguda, an eleventh century moral philosopher, relates the following story. A pious Jew in search of a livelihood left his family and journeyed to a foreign land. On his way he was met by an idolater and questioned why he worshipped idols. The heathen asked him in turn what he believed and worshipped. The Jew replied: 'I worship the creator of the Universe who cares for all His creatures.' On hearing this the gentile then said: 'What you do is contrary to your belief!' 'How so?' asked the Jew. 'Well,' answered the heathen, 'if what you believe is true, then your God could have provided for you in your own city and you need not have travelled to such a distant place.' On hearing this, the Jew returned home and never left his city again. (Introduction, Duties of the Heart, section on 'Trust in God').

There is a tannaitic statement which reads: 'Whoever has bread in his basket and says: "What am I going to eat tomorrow?" is but of little faith' (Sotah 48b). The Midrash goes on to state that every particle of creation has its own function and purpose and that God performs His designs through everything, even a serpent, insect or frog (Bereshit Rabbah 10).

Indeed, the mysterious ways of providence are beyond human understanding. Explaining the text: 'Behold, these are but the tips of His ways. What is the least we can understand about Him? Who can fathom the thunder of His mighty deeds?' (Job 26:14), Rabbi Huna said: 'All that you see are the outskirts of the Holy One's ways. If a man argues that he understands the order of the world, tell him: "You cannot even gauge the actions of a mortal king, do you expect to be able to fathom the ways of the King of Kings, the Holy One blessed be He?"' (ibid. 12).

The lesson we take from parshiot Thazria-Metzora is that God's providence is manifested in the daily events of life and that one should be careful in speech and action as the Psalmist reminds us: 'Who is the man that desired life, who loves days of seeing good? Guard your tongue from evil and your lips from speaking deceit' (34:17).

28

Acharei Mot – Kedoshim
HOLINESS CODE

And you shall keep My commandments and do them: I am the Lord.
And you shall not profane My holy Name, but I shall be
sanctified among the Children of Israel.

Leviticus 22:31, 32

THERE IS a collection of laws in chapters 17–26 in Leviticus which calls upon the Jewish people to be holy. Besides the quotation above, there are a number of times in the Chumash where the call is: 'You shall be holy for I the Lord your God am holy' or 'sanctify yourselves and be holy' or 'You shall be holy to me, for I am the Lord who sanctifies you.'

The Torah thus places the responsibility of every Jew to be careful not to profane the Name of God – '*Chillul Hashem*'. There is moreover, an equal duty to every Israelite to sanctify His Name – '*Kiddush Hashem*'.

Though there are some biblical commentators who are of the view that Leviticus chapter 22:32 is addressed to the Cohanim, the sons of Aaron, who were the guardians of the Sanctuary, the accepted opinion of our Rabbis is that it was addressed to the Jewish nation as a whole.

The Sages in Rabbinic Literature saw the terms '*Kiddush Hashem*' and '*Chillul Hashem*' – 'sanctification of the Divine Name' and 'defamation of the Divine Name' as significant concepts in Judaism offering man an active role in bestowing glory upon or detracting from the honour of God in the world.

The Gemara in Yoma 86a offers us examples of how the Divine Name may be sanctified or profaned. 'Abaye stated: "If someone studies scripture and Mishnah, and is honest in business, and speaks pleasantly to persons, what do people then say concerning him? Happy the father who taught him Torah; look how fine his ways are, how righteous his deeds! But if someone studies scripture and Mishnah, but is dishonest in business, and discourteous in his relations with people, what do people say about him? Woe unto him who studied Torah, woe to the father who taught him Torah."'

Man is responsible for sanctifying God's name in the world and this can be performed in private even when no-one is present. The Gemara in Sotah 36b states that Joseph, the son of Jacob, by restraining himself while alone in the face of temptation from Potiphar's wife, sanctified the Divine Name of the Holy One, blessed be He.

The Sages of the Talmud maintained that the ideal of Kiddush Hashem was to go beyond the strict requirements of the law and apply it in the area of ethical conduct. A classical example is the following story brought down in Midrash Deuteronomy Rabbah 3:3. On one occasion, Rabbi Shimon ben Shetach requested his disciples to purchase a camel from a gentile. On purchasing the animal they found a precious stone hanging around its neck and congratulated the Rabbi on his good fortune. 'Was the seller aware of this precious stone when he sold the animal?' asked Rabbi Shimon. On being told it was not so, the master returned it to the gentile. On receiving it back the gentile exclaimed: 'Blessed be the Lord, the God of Shimon ben Shetach.'

The concept of *Chillul Hashem* placed special standards of conduct on the teachers of Israel. The Sage Rab said; 'If I purchased meat from the butcher and did not pay for it immediately that would constitute, in his case, a desecration of the Divine Name.'

There is hardly anything more detrimental to Judaism than bringing His Name into disrepute nor anything greater than sanctifying His Name. Rabbi Yochanan ben Beroka stated: 'Whoever profanes the Name of God in secret will be punished in public, irrespective of whether it is done inadvertently or deliberately. On the other hand, those who in their everyday life risk their lives for the sake of God's Name, to them the words of the prophet Isaiah apply: "You are My servants, Israel, in whom I shall be glorified"' (49:3)

Let us conclude with the words of the Zohar: 'Happy are those who sanctify themselves with the holiness of the King and through their acts bring glory to His Name' (Emor).

29

Emor

ARISE AND GIVE LIGHT

You shall command the children of Israel that they bring to you pure olive oil beaten for the light, to cause a lamp to burn continually.

Leviticus 24:2

PARASHAT TERUMAH deals mainly with the building of a tabernacle and its contents. Among the sacred articles to be made was the menorah, the candelabrum, which was to be lit daily by the priest. Great prominence was given to the law of the golden seven-forked candlestick whose flames were fed by the purest oil from the olive. It was placed near the southern wall of the tabernacle in front of the curtain where the Ark reposed, to enhance the glory and splendour of the House of God through its continuous light.

Light is the emblem of Judaism. To keep the menorah lamps in purest order and brightness was one of the main duties of the priests, suggesting, no doubt, the diffusion of spiritual light and knowledge of God.

In Rabbinic literature, light as a symbol of Torah wisdom was to brighten up the path of man. The Midrash commentary on the words 'And you shall take' (ibid.) says 'Take for yourself for I (God) do not require any light.' Thus the words of the Torah give light to man when he is occupied with them. This may be compared to one who is standing in the dark. Unable to feel his way, he comes up against a stone and stumbles thereon, he meets other obstacles, falls and hurts himself. So it is with an ignorant person who lacks knowledge of Torah. He comes up against a transgression and falls. Whereas, he who is occupied with Torah has light before him; for as King Solomon said: 'Your words are a lamp to my feet' (Proverbs 4:12) (Shemot Rabbah 36:3).

The Bible commands the children of Israel to bring olive oil beaten for the menorah. Ibn Ezra comments on this: 'The oil for the menorah

90

was to be absolutely pure without any particles or sediments' Rashi further adds: 'The oil was made by pressing each olive gently until only one drop of pure oil emerged' (see Exodus 27:21, 2).

The Gemara in Menachot, in explaining Israel's suffering role, asks: 'Why is Israel likened to an olive tree? To teach us that just as the olive produces its oil by being pressed, so with Israel the nations of the world make us suffer in order that we return in service to God' (55b).

What this Gemara suggests is that it is only through oppression and persecution that the Jew returns to God and that prosperity and comfort create a distance between God and us. Interestingly enough, our teacher Moses in one of his farewell addresses to the Jewish people brought home this very message. He said: 'When you are in distress, and all things are come upon you, even in the latter days, then you will return to the Lord, your God, and listen to His voice' (Deuteronomy 4:30).

The questions one may ask are: Does Jewish history conform to this view? Is it only due to suffering and persecution that we have retained our adherence to Judaism? Is it the external pressures that enabled us to maintain our identity as God's chosen people? On the other hand, is there any other people that have been willing, to sacrifice all for their faith, as Jews have throughout the ages?

The answer lies in the paradox of the Jew. On the one hand, prosperity and comfort can create barriers between Israel and God. The prophet reminds Israel of the dangers of wealth and comfort. 'But Yeshurun waxed fat and kicked ... And he forsook God which made him, and held the Rock of his salvation' (ibid. 30:15). (This failing is not unique to Jews but is characteristic of all human beings.) On the other hand, as pointed out in the long, chequered history of our nation, there is no other people who have undergone suffering for the preservation of their faith as we have. As the People of the Book, throughout history we have survived paganism, Hellenism, the persecutions of the Church and other external dangers, proclaiming to our very last breath the declaration of our faith: 'Hear O Israel, the Lord our God, is One.'

Indeed, the Jewish people, like the Ner Tamid, the perpetual lamp of the menorah, continue by example to spread the moral teachings as given on Mount Sinai. Yes, in the words of the prophet Isaiah: 'You are

My witnesses, says the Lord, and My servant whom I have chosen'
(43:10). Yes, 'Arise and give light' has and will continue to be the
glorious call and privilege of the Jewish people bearing testimony to the
external wisdom of God and His Torah.

30

Behar-Bechukosai
EXILE AND REDEMPTION

And I will bring the land into desolation ... And I will
scatter you among the nations.

Leviticus 26: 32, 33

And the ransom of the Lord shall return and come forth singing to Zion,
and everlasting joy shall be upon their heads.

Isaiah 51:11

THE HISTORY of the Jewish people has been one long chain of alternative periods of exile and redemption, from the destruction of the First Temple in 586 BCE to the return to Eretz Yisrael from Babylon in 516 BCE, and from the destruction of the Second Temple in 70 CE, to the re-establishment of the State of Israel in 1948.

The Psalmist describes the feeling of the captives who had been forced to leave their country: 'By the rivers of Babylon, there we sat down, yes, we wept when we remembered Zion. For on the willows within it we hung up our harps. For there our captors requested words of song from us, and our tormentors asked for joyous music: "Sing us one of the songs of Zion." How shall we sing the Lord's song in a foreign land? If I forget you, O Jerusalem, let my right hand forget its skill. Let my tongue cleave to my palate, if I forget you not, if I fail to elevate Jerusalem above my chief joy' (137: 1–5).

The prophet Jeremiah, foretelling the destruction of the First Temple, whilst aware of this vision of a restored Zion, nonetheless saw that whilst in exile there was a future and hope for the people. He encouraged them, that though in '*galut*', God could be worshipped not just in Jerusalem but everywhere.

In this unique message written in a letter, the prophet expressed the special relationship between God and Israel with whom there could be communication in their new environment away from the soil of Israel.

In the name of God, he tells the captives: 'Build houses and settle, plant gardens and eat their produce. Take wives and bear sons and daughters; take wives for your sons and give your daughters husbands. Multiply there and be not diminished. And seek the peace of the city to which I have exiled you and pray to the Lord for it; for through its peace will you have peace' (Jeremiah 29: 4–7).

The effect of Jeremiah's words was immense. Such an idea had until now never been conceived or uttered by any other prophet. The Jews, he taught, could live outside the Holy Land, separated from the Temple and from sacred worship, yet remain faithful Jews without losing hope for a return to their homeland.

Commenting on the dispersion and exile of the Jewish nation, Hirsch explains the reason for our survival. 'Israel was driven into its great wandering through the wilderness of time and of people, possessing naught, its independence destroyed. To one blessed possession they clung throughout the wanderings, the Torah, and to one source of strength, God ... because of this they survived every storm, and every misfortune which threatened to overcome them. All this led to one thought, one idea: to regard the Torah as the one possession in life and the one God as the only God in their life' (Horev Section 23b).

With the birth of this new universalism, the exiled Jews in Babylon began to lay the foundations of Jewish national existence in the Galut. In the birth of this new message, lands of exile could turn into homelands, with no contradiction between love of Zion and the motherland and attachment to other countries where Jews would dwell. Moreover, attachment to the observance of God's laws as contained in the Torah would enable them to remain faithful without losing hope of a future restoration in Eretz Yisrael.

In the Book of Ezra we read of how seventy years later, fulfilment of Jewish prophecy was first brought to fruition by the overthrow of the Babylonian empire by the Persian King Cyrus in 539 BCE following which he gave permission for the Jews by an edict to return to their homeland and build a Temple in Jerusalem. 'Thus says Cyrus, King of Persia, issued in a proclamation throughout his kingdom and in writing: "Whoever is among you ... let him go up to Jerusalem ... and build the Temple of the Lord God of Israel, in Jerusalem. And whoever remains

... bestow gifts of silver and gold, of valuables and of animals together with their contribution for the Temple of God'" (Ezra 1:2–7). Unfortunately, because of interference from Israel's enemies, it was only two decades after the publication of this edict, in 521 BCE, that the Second Temple was finally built in the reign of Artaxerxes.

Following the loss of the Second Temple, the Jewish nation's intense love for the vision of Zion restored anew never faded. This dream was finally achieved in our days with the return of our people to our homeland. Our prayer is: May we be worthy to see the ultimate prophecy of Isaiah fulfilled: 'Come let us go to the Mountain of the Lord, to the Temple of the God of Jacob, and He will teach us of His ways and we will walk in His paths. For from Zion will the Torah come forth, and the word of the Lord from Jerusalem' (2:2, 3).

31

Bemidbar
IN HIS IMAGE

And the Lord spoke unto Moses ... saying: 'Take you the sum of all the
congregation of the children of Israel, by their families ...
by number of the names, every male.'

Numbers 1:2

A MONTH after the erection of the Tabernacle in the wilderness, Moses is commanded to take a census of all adult males above the age of twenty. Rashi, Prince of commentators, explains that because of God's love for the Bnei Yisrael, he counts them frequently. He counted them when they left Egypt (Exodus 12:37), after the sin of the making of the Golden Calf (ibid. 38:26) and when He came to cause His Divine Presence to abide among them, He counted them (the opening words of this parasha).

Whilst the numbering of the nation was undoubtedly important both in regard to the growth of the nation which, when they first arrived, consisted of just seventy people and now was six hundred and three thousand, five hundred and fifty (see v. 46), it is the special relationship which God has with us His people to which Rashi draws our attention.

The question that one needs to ask is: what is the significance of the Hebrew word 'Naso'? Though it is translated in our quotation of Numbers 1:1 as 'Take', the literal meaning of the word is 'lift up'. So what is the significance of 'lifting up the heads of the Jewish people'?

Let us consider how in ancient times people lived. Basically, they were ruled by kings, pharaohs and men in power. These people ruled the population and had control over the lives of the poor and weak. Consider the Pyramids and the Tower of Babel. They were built by slaves and the masses of ordinary people. In the Midrash we find a description of those Tower builders and of the efficient manner in which they operated. Thus, we are told that if a man dropped dead, no-one would pay any attention but if a brick broke, they would sit down and weep (*Pirkei De Rabbi Eliezer*).

The Torah, on the other hand, in describing the numbering of the Israelites, refers to the census as the lifting up of the individual; to teach that every person, irrespective of class or colour, rich or poor, is equally important and precious in the eyes of God. Created in the image of God, the Bible stresses that all individuals are equal in the eyes of our Creator and each counts as a member of the nation.

The Malbim explains that the text 'by number of the names, every male' meant that the individual, each man, wrote his name and gave it to Moses. There was therefore no need to count the people themselves, for each man stated his name and wrote it in a register. In this manner, every man of age, great or small, prince or commoner, was equal before God.

The sacredness of the human personality is, in the eyes of the Torah, the cornerstone of all human relations. The Rabbis considered the life of a slave to be as sacred as that of a free man and there was to be no difference between a king and a slave in the eyes of the law. In the *Mishnah Sanhedrin* 4:5, we are told: 'A single man was first created so that no man should say to his fellow: "My ancestor was greater than your ancestor".'

Interestingly, our Sages, whilst emphasising the many royal prerogatives given to a king in Israel, yet held that he was not to be looked upon as a superhuman being but was, in the eyes of the law, to be treated as an ordinary human being. Thus, if he transgressed in any of the positive or negative prohibitions or commandments, he was to be treated in all matters as an ordinary man (Tosefta 4:2).

The sacredness of every human life can perhaps be best reflected in the fact that legal rights were extended to all alike. The Torah exhorts: 'You shall not show partiality to the poor man, nor pay respect to the person of might, but in righteousness shall you judge your neighbour' (Leviticus 19:15). Indeed, God's love to all individuals is based not upon the social structure of society but upon our equality in the presence of God. Yes, we are all special, each created with a task and a mission in the world.

The standard of human equality is best reflected in the following story. It once happened that a slave of King Yannai killed a man. Simon ben Shetach, who was head of the Sanhedrin, sent a message to the King: 'Your slave has killed a person and you and your slave must appear before the court.' Thereupon, Yannai sent his slave to the Sages to be tried. The Sages then sent him a message: 'You too must come here'. Yannai then came to the court and sat down. Then Simon ben Shetach said: 'King Yannai, stand on your feet and let the witnesses testify against you, for you are not standing before us but before the Holy One who created the world' (Sanhedrin 19a).

Similarly, one finds that the standard of equality applied to a *Kohen Gadol* – a High Priest – who violated a positive or negative command is to treat him like any other person in law (*Maimonides, Yad HaHazakah, Yesodei Torah* 5:4). The reason for this is that in the eyes of God all men are considered equal.

From the above one learns that despite the royal prerogatives grant to a king and high priest the Sages emphasised that one must always be under the rulership of God and that in the eyes of God all are equal.

32

Naso

THE SOURCE OF ALL BLESSING

The Lord lift up His countenance upon you, and give you peace.

Numbers 6:26

Depart from evil and do good; seek peace and pursue it.

Psalm 34:15

ONE of the most beautiful blessings in the Bible is the benediction recited daily in Temple times by the priests. Today in Israel, and in some congregations in the diaspora, this custom is still performed in synagogues during the morning service. In its threefold form it is a petition for material and spiritual success with which the priests are instructed to bless Israel on behalf of God, the source of all gifts.

There is no greater source of divine blessing in the world than peace. Rabbi Simon ben Halafta, a second century Tanna, taught: 'The Holy One, blessed be He, found no better source of blessing for Israel than peace as it is said: "The Lord will give strength to His people, the Lord will bless His people with peace" (Psalm 29:11): (Uktzin 3:12).

Another Talmudic Sage, Hezekiah, said: 'Israel received the Torah at Sinai through unity and peace.' Throughout the travels of Israel in the desert, we are told 'and they journeyed', 'and they encamped' but at Sinai it says 'Israel encamped' in the singular as a people united to receive the Torah (Midrash Vayikra Rabbah 9). Thus, the Torah was given against a background of peace and unity. The prophets also cherished peace and considered it as the most important part of the Messianic age when mankind will be united.

The importance and promotion of peace is further found in today's parsha. Twelve times we are told of the gifts offered by the princes of the tribes at the consecration of the Tabernacle. Since their gifts were all identical, what was the need for the Torah to repeat time and time again their offerings? The answer is that since there was unity among the princes with no one wishing to outrival the others, their gifts are written down separately. Rabbi Hirsch, writing on the importance of peace, writes: 'When a person is friendly and rejoices in the success and well-being of his fellow man and enjoys his prosperity as his own, the picture of peace which God intended when he created the world will be achieved' (Horev Section 388).

The following story shows the lengths to which one must be prepared to go in the interests of peace. Rabbi Meir used to lecture every Shabbat eve in the synagogue. There was one woman who used to attend his discourses regularly. On one occasion, his lecture was unusually long and when she arrived home the Sabbath candles had burnt out. 'Where have you been?' asked the husband. She replied: 'I was at the lecture of the Rabbi.' The husband did not believe her and being suspicious, suggested that she go and spit in the rabbi's face. In order to appease her husband, she went to Rabbi Meir who, on being told of her husband's wish, said to her that his eyes were hurting him but would be cured if she spat in his eye seven times. She did as she was requested. The Rabbi then told her: 'Go and tell your husband that you demanded that I spit at the Rabbi once, but I did so seven times' (Jerusalem Talmud Sotah 1:4).

Indeed the pursuit of peace and its promotion was one of the traits of Aaron, the high priest. Hillel used to say: 'Be of Aaron's disciples – loving peace and pursuing peace, loving men and drawing them near to Torah' (Avot 1:12). Explaining the text: 'The law of truth was in his mouth, and unrighteousness was not found in his lips; he walked with Me in Peace and uprightness, and did turn many away from iniquity' (Malachi 2:6), it is stated that when Aaron took a walk he would make a special point of greeting a wicked man. Again, when two men quarrelled with each other, Aaron would go out of his way to make peace (Avot de Rabbi Natan).

It is further related of Rabbi Yochanan ben Zakkai that no man ever gave him greeting first, even a heathen in the street. The Sage Abaye said: 'One should always strive to be on the best terms with family, relatives and all men and even with the heathen in the street' (Berachot 17a). It is related that the Babylonian Sage Abaye used to say: 'One should at all times strive to be on the best terms with everyone so that he will find favour in heaven and on earth' (ibid.).

Indeed, there is not a blessing or prayer in our liturgy, be it the Shemoneh Esrei, Kaddish or Grace after Meals, which does not conclude with the prayer for peace. Peace, writes Maimonides, is the crowning blessing of the golden age promised Israel and mankind. 'In that era there will be neither famine nor war, neither jealousy nor strife, goodwill shall be spread everywhere and all mankind will know the Lord' (Yad Hachazakah, Melachim 12:5).

Among the various Talmudic statements about peace, let us quote yet another: 'All the laws of the entire Torah were decreed because they are the ways which foster harmony! For it is written Her (the Torah's) ways are ways of pleasantness, and all Her paths are peaceful' (proverbs 3:17) (Gittin 59:b).

33

Beha'alotecha

FAITH

For six years you may sow your field ... and you may gather in its crop.
But the seventh year shall be a complete rest for the land.

Leviticus 25:3, 4

THE PARSHA commences with the laws of *Shemittah*. The Torah commands us that whilst for six years we are permitted to work and benefit from the land of Israel, on the seventh year we are to cease working on it. By letting the land rest on the seventh – Sabbatical – year, we show that the land is not ours but God's. By doing so, we further show our faith that He is the provider of all our needs and that the sixth-year crop will be so abundant that it will provide for the next three years until the ninth year.

The Torah assures us that in return for observing the Shemittah there will be a blessing of much prosperity (as a reward for such faith in God). Let us quote the text: 'If you say: what will we eat on the seventh year? Behold! We will not sow and not gather in our crops! I will order My blessing for you in the sixth year and it will yield a crop sufficient for the three-year period. You will sow in the eighth year, but you will eat from the old crop, until the ninth year' (ibid. 20–22).

The Shemittah year is a wonderful lesson in faith in God's blessings and a reminder that the fulfilment of this mitzvah is an open miracle of receiving the reward of a triple crop in the sixth year.

Faith in God is a fundamental principle of Judaism. The history of the Jewish people, beginning with the Patriarchs, Abraham, Isaac and Jacob, is based on faith and it makes us the bearers of the divine message to all mankind. Our Sages say that it was the great faith that the Israelites demonstrated at the Reed Sea, when the Holy Spirit came to rest upon them, which led them to produce a song of praise (see Mekhilta, Beshallach). Similarly, we are told that when the Children of

Israel learnt in Egypt of their forthcoming deliverance from their afflictions: 'The people believed that the Lord remembered and saw their sufferings, and they bowed down their heads and prostrated themselves' (Exodus 4:31).

Emunah – (faith) – denotes absolute belief in Divine Providence, in God's unfailing goodness to all and it is considered an essential part of a commandment of the Torah. The Gemara in Makkot 23b–24a states: Six hundred and thirteen commandments were given to Moses. Then came King David and established eleven ethical and moral requirements as the basis for their fulfilment. The prophet Isaiah established the basis for their fulfilment upon six ethical requirements. Later, the prophet Micah established the basis for fulfilment of the Torah's commandment upon three ethical requirements. The prophet Isaiah again came and established the basis for fulfilment of the Torah's commandments on two ethical requirements. The prophet Habakkuk established them upon one ethical requirement – 'The righteous man shall live by his faith.' (For a full understanding of the requirements as taught by King David and the Prophets, see the Gemara where their teachings are expounded in detail.) Rabbi Hirsch in his work '*Horeb*', speaking of trust in God, writes: 'Emunah means holding fast to God even when His ruling hand does not show itself in the fulfilment of His promises.'

One question which has puzzled the minds of people from the beginning of history is: Why do some good people suffer, while some bad people prosper? Why does the law of reward and punishment not correspond with what is good or evil? In the Bible, Job, we are told, endured a series of sufferings, but does not find an answer to his questions. The reason is that our faculties are limited: we cannot grasp the ways of God. There are many things we would wish to understand but, as the Bible puts it: 'It is far beyond us.' Ultimately, we must submit to faith in God and believe that His ways are perfect and that He knows best. See also Gemara Berachot 5a and 7a for a lengthy discussion on this subject.

The Hebrew word '*emunah*' which is commonly translated as 'faith' also means trust, reliance and holding fast to God's ruling power. The Talmud records a Tannaitic statement: 'Whoever has bread in his basket and says what will I eat tomorrow is but of little faith' (Sotah

48b). We thus see that 'faith' in God must be the basis of life and offers us the strength and courage to continue in times of joy and sorrow. The proof of 'emunah' lies in our past history when, throughout the centuries, our ancestors endured insult, contempt, misery and even death. Yet with all this we, their descendants, still live by the teachings of the Torah and faith in the all-powerful and beneficent God. The Psalmist expresses this aptly: 'I chose the path of faith. Your judgments I set before me' (119:30).

34

Shelach Lecha

THE MISSION

And the Lord spoke to Moses, saying: Send men that they may spy out the land of Canaan that I give to the children of Israel.

Numbers 13, 1, 2

HE ISRAELITES were nearing the borders of the land of Canaan. This was the land promised to their forefathers and 'flowing with milk and honey'. Yet, despite the wonders they had experienced, both before their departure from Egypt and in the desert, they assembled around Moses with the request to send out spies to scout out the land.

The Midrash records that Moses was in a dilemma. Did they not show lack of faith in God's promise to bring them into the Promised Land? What should he do? If he acceded to their wishes, did it not demonstrate lack of trust in God? If, however, he refused to listen to their request, it would confirm their fears that the country was unconquerable. So Moses consulted God on this matter and was told: 'Send spies if you so desire. I do not command you to do so' (Tanchuma).

The Bible records that Moses chose twelve men, one from each tribe, for this mission and said to them: 'See the land, what it is, and the people that dwell in it, whether strong or weak, whether they are few or many ... and be you of good courage, and bring of the fruit of the land' (Numbers 13:18, 20).

Some of our commentators ask the following questions. Why did God, on being asked by Moses, permit such an expedition? Secondly, were the spies on a voluntary mission, or engaged in the performance of a mitzvah? Rashi, quoting a Gemara, states that God did not command Moses to send spies, and left the choice to him (Sotah 34b). The reason why God did not prevent such an expedition is that the Almighty does

105

not prevent a man from going his own way. To quote our Sages: *'Baderech she'adam rotzeh lelech, molichim oto'*. (A person is led on the path he wishes to go) (Makkot 10b). Thus, in accordance with the doctrine of free will, man is permitted to follow his own desires in the hope that he will succeed.

The Ramban, on the other hand, is of the opinion that though not commanded by God they were on a mission and part of God's plan. He writes: 'For God desires for His righteous sake that the emissaries be engaged in a mitzvah with all the tribes being represented, and by great men, in order that they may be saved from lack of faith.'

Similarly, one is told in a midrash on the text: 'Send if you wish.' There is nothing dearer to the Holy One, blessed be He, than a messenger who is sent to perform a mitzvah and devotes his entire being to succeed in his mission. The only men, one finds, who were sent for such a purpose and devoted themselves to succeed in it, were the two spies whom Joshua sent. But those that Moses sent were unfortunately wicked. How do we know this? From what is written in parsha Shelach Lecha Anashim' (Bemidbar Rabbah 16:1).

The doctrine of free will, the ability granted to the individual to choose between alternative possibilities of action, is considered as a basic principle of Judaism. The prophet Moses, before leaving this world, clearly states: 'I have placed life and death before you, the blessing and the curse; choose life, so that you and your descendants may live' (Deuteronomy 30:19). Rabbi Akiva further declared: 'Though everything is foreseen by God, yet free will is granted to man' (Avot 3:19). The doctrine of free will, ascribing to every person the right to freedom and ability to choose between alternative possibilities of action is considered a basic principle of Judaism.

Maimonides saw the Jewish doctrine of free will as the pillar of the Torah and the divine commandments, but that while normally a man is free to choose, he may forfeit his freedom if he abuses it. He writes: 'Every person is capable of being as upright as Moses, or as wicked as Jeroboam, wise of foolish, kind or cruel. The Creator does not predetermine whether a man should be good or evil, as the foolish astronomers falsely allege ... for as Jeremiah said "From God does not proceed evil or good" (Mishne Torah, Repentance 5:2).'

The ten spies, by bringing back an evil report, showed not just a lack of faith in God but also in the moral strength of the people. History has taught us that the report these spies brought back, of brute force and physical power of nations, do not truly constitute the strength of a nation. The real test in life is those spiritual and moral values which lead to success. When the time came for Israel, forty years later, to conquer the Promised Land, Joshua and Caleb, who praised the land saying: 'You shall not fear the people of the land, for they are our bread ... Hashem is with us. Do not fear them' proved to be right; for all the alleged terror of the inhabitants and its giants soon melted away. Yes, the conquest of the land was a long and arduous struggle but ultimately the result was never in doubt. The lesson is clear. No matter what obstacles and difficulties arise in life, with trust in God one can overcome them.

35

Korach

DANGERS OF SELF-INTEREST

*All the congregation are holy, every one of them; why then do you
lift yourselves above the assembly of the Lord?*

Numbers 16:3

REVOLUTIONS that occur in countries around the world are no
new phenomenon. They have taken place since time
immemorial and undoubtedly will happen again. There are
many reasons for this. At times, people rebel against a dictator or unjust
government when they believe they suffer under laws passed against
themselves. Corruption may also be a reason for revolt, whose object is
to remove those in power by putting in their place a leader or men of
integrity.

A revolt may also occur for ideological reasons when people feel
the need to overthrow the ruling class because of political, economic
and social rules that are not in their interest. Lastly a rebellion may start
because of the personal motivation of an individual or group driven by a
desire for power. They are guided by jealousy and ambition and will go
to any lengths to achieve their objective.

This week's scriptural portion tells the story of a rebellion initiated
by one who succeeded in rallying two hundred and fifty leaders to
oppose the authority of Moses' leadership. Korach, the one behind the
uprising, was from the tribe of Levi and was aggrieved for not being
appointed to high office by Moses in the distribution of honours. Since
he could not charge Moses with being a despot, he based his challenge
on ideological grounds. As a true demagogue he posed as champion of
the people saying, 'All the congregation are holy ... why then do you lift
yourself above the assembly of the Lord?'

Rashi, quoting a midrash, states that Korach undertook to show that
Moses' religious rulings were ridiculous and not logical. He appeared

with his associates before Moses dressed in four-cornered garments made entirely of blue wool and asked whether they required fringes. 'Yes,' replied Moses. They then mockingly said: 'Do you admit that one cord of blue in a tallit is sufficient to exempt it from the law of being ritually correct? Why then should it be necessary to insert a cord of blue in a tallit which is made entirely of blue?' (Tanchuma, Korach). (The midrash there offers many other questions which they posed to Moses in the hope of discrediting his decisions.)

Moses realised that any counter-arguments from him would be futile since Korach and his followers were motivated not by a desire for truth but by jealousy and by ambition. The only way to justify his position was if the matter were decided directly by the intervention of God. The dispute was finally settled by the death of Korach, whereupon his associates were swallowed up into the ground upon which they stood.

Pirke Avot says: 'Any dispute for the sake of heaven will have enduring value, but any dispute not for the sake of heaven will not have enduring value. What is an example of a dispute for the sake of heaven? The dispute between Hillel and Shammai. What is an example of one not for the sake of heaven? The dispute of Korach and all his company.' (5:20).

The Malbim, a nineteenth-century commentator, explains that a controversy for the sake of heaven is one where the individuals or groups genuinely desire to uncover the truth and whose motives are pure. A controversy pursued for unholy ends is one where they are motivated by jealousy or self-interest.

Hirsch, in his section dealing with self-appraisal, writes: 'There is no more effective protection against the danger of defying the person than a proper self-appraisal ... If you feel yourself to have been assigned by God to the station in which you were born, in order to execute His will in that post, in that circle, with those means, in that space of time ... then with that consciousness and that spirit you stand on a level with the most brilliant, most gifted creatures. In that consciousness you see all creatures on a level, all performing the task assigned to them by God, all servants round the throne of God' (Horev 19).

Before concluding, it is important to understand the biblical view of leadership. This is not one of status, or power but of service in bringing others closer to God. On the appointment of a Jewish king, it says: 'It shall be when he sits on the throne of his kingdom, he shall write for himself two copies of the Law in a book ... And it shall be with him, and he shall read from it all the days of his life, that he may learn to fear the Lord his God ... that his heart be not lifted up above his brethren.' (Deuteronomy 17: 18–20).

Moses was the humblest of all men and is called '*eved Hashem*' (servant of God). Leadership, in Jewish teachings, implies humility, respect for others and guiding others to a noble and virtuous life. This was the difference between Korach, who saw leadership as conferring power and honour, and Moses, who dedicated his actions to the service of God. This idea of service is illustrated in the Gemara Horayot. When the exilarch Rabban Gamliel decided to appoint two Rabbis to high office, he said to them: 'Do you imagine I offer you rulership? It is servitude that I offer you.'

36

Chukkat-Balak

AARON THE PEACE MAKER

When all the congregation saw that Aaron was dead,
they wept for Aaron thirty days.

Numbers 20:29

SHALOM is the word one most frequently hears in Israel. In Jewish literature the word 'Shalom' has a wider meaning than the English equivalent 'peace'; for it could also signify divine grace, protection, friendliness and favour. In Jeremiah, God's grace (shalom) is explained as kindness and mercy (16:5). Similarly, in the priestly blessing (see Numbers 6:24–26) 'peace' means favour, kindheartedness , friendship and grace.

In the Talmud, peace is considered the most ideal way of life. 'The Holy One, blessed be He, found no vessel more worthy of retaining a blessing within it than peace,' (Mishna Uktzin 3:12). The famous Hillel used to say: 'Love peace and strive for peace' (Pirke Avot 1:12) and there is an ancient tradition going back to the time of Moses that the prophet Elijah will come to the world to bring peace, as it is said: 'I will send you Elijah the prophet ... and he will turn the heart of the fathers to the children, and the heart of the children to the fathers.' (Malachi 3:24)

In Rabbinic teachings Aaron, the brother of Moses and Miriam, is the ideal peacemaker and is referred to by Hillel as one who loved peace and pursued peace. It is related that if he learned that two people had quarrelled, he would do everything possible to make peace between them.

In the early chapters of Exodus, we are told that though appointed as a spokesman to Israel and Pharaoh, Aaron was assigned a role subordinate to Moses. When the ten plagues befell the Egyptians, one finds that he acted jointly with Moses in bringing about the first plague, operated alone in the second and third plagues and participated again with Moses in the sixth and eighth plagues.

In the incident of the 'manna' when the people murmured against Moses and Aaron, Aaron was once again called upon by Moses to 'take a jar and put an omerful of manna and lay up before the Lord' (Exodus 16:33) as a reminder of the forty years during which the children of Israel consumed it in the wilderness.

Before Moses' ascent to Mount Sinai to receive the '*shnai luchot ha'edut*' (two tablets of the testimony) he placed Aaron and Chur in charge. When Moses did not appear at the appointed time (the people had misunderstood the forty day period of return – see Rashi ibid. 32:1), they demanded from Aaron a visible god. In the hope of gaining time till Moses would arrive, he yielded to the popular demand by asking them to give up their silver and gold, which, on being melted, took the shape of a calf. Moses, after his descent and on seeing the calf with the people dancing, broke the tablets beneath the mount. The participation of Aaron in such an offence caused Moses to hold him culpable for this act. He says to Aaron: 'What did this people to you, that you have brought a great sin upon them?' (ibid. v.21). The Torah states that God was very angry with Aaron and wished to destroy him but he was saved by virtue of Moses' intercession on his behalf (see Deuteronomy 9:20).

Despite Aaron's involvement in the golden calf episode, he was not disqualified from the priesthood and became the founder of an hereditary priesthood in which he served until his death. In Aggadic literature, Aaron is praised by our Sages for his kindness and love for his fellow men. He was furthermore free of envy that Moses, his younger brother, was the leader of the nation and that he was assigned a subordinate role to that of Moses. The Midrash records that because of this, he was rewarded by becoming the '*Cohen Gadol*' (High Priest) and wore the '*Urim Vetummim*' (the breastplate) (Tanchuma Exodus 27).

Aaron is regarded as the prototype of the ideal peacemaker and there is a detailed account of the manner in which he devoted himself to achieve this. In Avot de Rabbi Natan, it is said that Aaron's desire to strive for peace led him never to reproach anyone by telling him that he had sinned and this kindness led many a sinner to reform. When Aaron died, it was said of him: 'The law of truth was in his mouth, and unrighteousness was not found on his lips; he walked with Me in peace and uprightness, and did turn many away from iniquity.' (Malachi 2:6)

Indeed, Aaron is the ideal peace-maker and everyone is called upon to be a disciple of Aaron, loving peace and pursuing peace, loving his fellow man and drawing them near to the Torah.

37

Pinchas

JEREMIAH'S MESSAGE

The word of the Lord came to me saying: 'Before I formed you and before you came forth from the womb, I sanctified you; I have appointed you a prophet to the nations.' Then said I: 'O Lord God! Behold I cannot speak; for I am a child'

Jeremiah 1:4–6

THE HAFTAROT selected to be read between the seventeenth of Tammuz and the ninth of Av all deal with the causes that led to the destruction of the First Temple and the exile to Babylon. The prophet Jeremiah who lived at that time received a call to warn Israel of their defection from God and the dire consequences that would follow.

The causes of the impending fall of the Jewish state were the prevailing lack of morals, the scorn of justice and the oppression of the poor and defenceless. The purpose of his message was not one calling for the destruction of the people but for the preservation of the core of the nation which would remain faithful to the word of God.

The prophet recalls its earlier history. When God remembers Israel's attachment and devotion to Him, he proclaims in God's name: 'I remember unto you the affection of your youth. The attachment of love when you went after Me in the wilderness, into a land that was not sown' (ibid 2:2). It was such love that caused them to follow the call of God with unfounded confidence that set apart Israel from the nations, as the first fruits were set apart for the priests. Though now estranged from their true calling and mission their destiny still remains eternal.

However, Israel, in not reminding itself of the blessings that emanate from fulfilling God's will, were now disloyal in their duty and worldly destiny. All those in authority, responsible for the welfare of the nation, have failed in their duty. The priests whose task was to offer a correct direction did not do so and the men of Jewish learning who had knowledge of the Law did not act in the spirit of its teachings. They therefore could not open the minds and hearts of the people to God and stand as examples and defenders of the Torah. The degeneration had taken such deep root for even 'they prophesied by Baal and walked after things that do not profit' (ibid. 8). The admonishing words with which the prophet warned Israel right until the last hour, identifying their defection from God on account of their prevailing lack of morals, the worship of sensuality, the scorn of justice, the misuse of power and the oppression of the poor and defenceless as being the causes of the impending collapse of the Jewish State.

Moreover, Israel, unique among the nations, by its own free will had changed and forgotten the past personal experiences: such as the mighty acts of God in their deliverance from Egypt, the parting of the Red Sea, the Revelation at Sinai and the forty years where they were provided for in the desert. Having forgotten the ever-fresh source of living waters, that is, Almighty God, they had exchanged their glory for things that did not profit.

The prophet in speaking of Israel's continued defection dealt further with their faithlessness in relying on allies who had proved to be their enemies. He reminded them of the folly of making foreign alliances with Egypt and Assyria which had not brought them any profit. The misfortunes arising from their wickedness should have corrected them and led them to the right path. 'Your own wickedness should correct you, and your backslidings should reprove you! O perceive and see that it is an evil and bitter thing that you have forsaken the Lord your God' (ibid. 19).

There was nothing new in the announcement of doom which Jeremiah uttered. In his call for repentance, he reminded Israel of God's love for them and ended his message on a note of hope. To quote his words: 'If you will, O Israel, return to Me, and if you put away your detestable things out of My sight, and will not waver. And if you will swear as the Lord lives in exercising truth, justice and loving kindness; then the nations will be blessed in Him and will find glory in Him' (ibid. 4:1, 2). Yes, with this comforting optimism the prophet ends with the outlook of well-being and happiness that will blossom out far beyond the Jewish future into the whole world.

38

Mattos Massei

ILLUSORY OR REAL VALUES

And the children of Reuben and the children of Gad had a very great multitude of cattle, and when they saw the land of Gezer, and the land of Gilead, behold the place was a place for cattle.

Numbers 32:1

THE TRIBES of Reuben and Gad had become exceedingly wealthy in the war against Midian. Having acquired large herds of cattle, they desired to settle on the other side of the Jordan rather than move to the Promised Land. Approaching Moses, Eleazar and the princes of the congregation, they said: 'The country which the Lord smote before the congregation of Israel is a land of cattle, and your servants have cattle. If we have found grace in your sight, let this land be given to your servants for a possession and bring us not over the Jordan' (ibid. 2-5).

On hearing this, they received a torrent of rebuke from Moses. Had they learnt nothing from the stories of the spies who through their evil report caused the people to wander in the desert for forty years? Now that they were about to enter and conquer the land promised to them and their forefathers, were they not forsaking their brethren in their responsibility? 'Shall your brethren go to war and shall you sit here? And wherefore will you turn away the heart of the children of Israel from going over into the land which the Lord had given them?'

On hearing Moses' strong denunciation, they clarified their request by stating that they were ready to join the other tribes in the wars against the Canaanites, but before journeying with their brethren they would erect cities for their families and stables for their cattle on Transjordan.

We are told that Moses accepted their proposal on the condition that they fulfilled their promise.

In the Book of Joshua, it is stated that the two and a half tribes fulfilled their obligation. 'Joshua said to them: "You have observed all that Moses, the servant of the Lord had commanded you ... Now go and return to your tents, to the land of your possession ... Only take heed to fulfil the commandments and the Torah which Moses the servant of the Lord commanded you"' (24:1–4).

Unfortunately, history informs us that these tribes who settled in Transjordan and separated themselves from their brethren were the first to go into exile. 'And they broke faith with the God of their fathers and went astray after the gods of the people of the land, whom God destroyed before them. And the God of Israel stirred up the spirit of Pul, King of Assyria, and the spirit of Tiglat-Pileser, King of Assyria, and he carried them away, even the Reubenites and the Gadites, and the half tribe of Menasseh' (I Chronicles 5:25, 26).

The Midrash has its commentary on its attitude to material success. When the gifts of God are utilised for a noble purpose they are a blessing: otherwise they can be a curse. 'Three gifts were created in the world: wisdom, strength and wealth. If a person is privileged to one of these he can attain as his own the most precious things in the whole world. If he is privileged to possess strength, he has attained everything; if he is privileged to possess wealth, he has attained everything. When does this apply? When they are gifts of heaven and come through the observance of the Torah, but the strength and wealth by themselves are nought, as King Solomon says: "I returned, and saw under the sun that the race is not to the swift, nor the battle to the strong, neither yet bread to the wise, nor yet riches to men of understanding, nor yet favour to men of skill, but time and chance happens to them all" (Ecclesiastes 9:11).

'Furthermore, two wise men arose in this world, one in Israel and one among the gentiles – Ahitophel in Israel and Balaam among the nations of the world – and both were destroyed from the world. Similarly, two strong men arose in the world – Samson in Israel and Goliath among the nations of the world – and both of them were destroyed from the world. Again, two rich men arose in the world – Korach in Israel and Haman among the nations of the world – and both of them were destroyed from the world. Why? Because their gifts were not from God but they snatched it for themselves. Similarly, in the case of the children of Gad and the children of Reuben, you find they were wealthy, possessing large numbers of cattle, but dazzled by their success they separated from their brethren and were lost to the nation.' (Rabbah Numbers 22:7).

Hillel used to say: 'Separate yourself not from the community' (Ethics of the Fathers 2:5) and Rabbi Hirsch taught: 'Alas if in the pursuit of wealth and property you lose your higher self, if you distance yourself from the spirit and duty of being part of Israel in order to snatch at wealth ... No, this is not the will of God nor the purpose of your mission as an Israelite' (Horev 525).

The attitude of Judaism to wealth is clear and correct. Wealth is an instrument for good if used wisely and spent for the welfare of others, but if misused can lead to disunity and harm. Man's duty is to use God's blessings as an instrument to achieve the potentialities for human elevation, philanthropy and spiritual attainments. Moreover, the fate that overtook the two and a half tribes that stayed on the other side of the Jordan and were lost in exile is a constant reminder of the importance of not separating oneself from the historical Divine mission of a united people.

39

Devarim
THE VOICE OF WISDOM

*And now Israel, listen to the statutes and to the ordinances, which I teach
you to do them ... for this is your wisdom and your
understanding in the sight of the people.*
Deuteronomy 4:1, 6

*Happy the person who finds wisdom ... for she is
a tree of life to them that lay hold unto her.*
Proverbs 3:13,17

MOSES, the lawgiver, had brought Israel at the end of forty
years to the borders of the Holy Land. In his first discourse,
he calls upon his people to observe the Divine Law which,
due to its unique moral and ethical teachings, would lead the nations of
the world to say: 'Surely this great nation is a wise and understanding
people' (ibid. 6).

Throughout Jewish history, there arose prophets and seers who
devoted themselves to the study of 'wisdom'. In time, there appeared a
number of 'wisdom books' which came down in the form of three
remarkable ones called Proverbs, Ecclesiastes and Job. These works are
contained in the Tanach and are known as 'Wisdom Literature'.

The moment one reads the Book of Proverbs, for example, one is
struck by the fact that one is being addressed personally. 'My son, hear
the instructions of your father' (1:8). 'My son, if you will receive my
words' (2:1). Here, the teacher does not command nor legislate. The
only authority to which he lays claim is that conferred by age,
experience and learning.

Essentially, wisdom was not seen as a natural gift but something
which had to be acquired through learning and discipline. Wisdom
could be attained, rewarding those who seek it: 'If you seek her as silver

and search for her as for hidden treasure then you will understand the fear and knowledge of God' (ibid. 2:4, 5). Such divine wisdom would direct one's path and protect one from evil (ibid. 3:6). The standard of ethics which the teachers set was high but so also was the reward.

There were two distinct methods of instruction: one of counselling and the other of training; and whilst wisdom was open to all, young and old, it would not be attained spontaneously. It was a parent's duty to instruct and, when necessary, correct the disobedient child. 'For though you beat him with the rod, he will not die' (ibid. 23:13).

In a similar manner, a teacher urges his pupil to follow the guidance which his parents have given him as it is always well-intentioned. 'Hear, my son, the instruction of your father and forsake not the teaching of your mother' (ibid. 1:8). (Interestingly, Rashi explains this text homiletically, defining father as God and mother as the nation of Israel, calling on the young to obey the precepts revealed by God and the laws of the community based on tradition.)

The 'Wisdom Books' of the Bible all had a common theme. Man's wisdom was to follow in the path of divine wisdom and conform to the will of God. These wise men held that knowledge and practice of wisdom as a distinct way of life would make such a person more capable of offering advice and leadership for a sound and efficient running of government and society. Such a person would at all times be aware that 'The fear of the Lord, that is wisdom; and to depart from evil is understanding' (ibid. 28:28). He would have learned that the divine plan in creation called for a society in which the rights of others were respected, and concern for those less fortunate was maintained in an atmosphere of general kindness.

It will be seen from this that true wisdom was a very practical thing. It had to do with life more than thought, with the nature of reality and the ability to lead a good and happy life. Indeed, as Scripture says: 'Her ways are ways of pleasantness, and all her paths are peace. She is a tree of life to them that lay hold upon her and happy is everyone that retains her' (3:17, 18).

In Ethics of the Fathers, seven traits characterise an uncultured person and a wise man. A Sage does not speak before one who is wiser than he; does not interrupt the words of his fellow; does not answer impetuously; he questions according to the subject matter and answers to the point. He deals with first things first and last things last. Regarding that which he has not understood, he says: 'I do not understand it, and he acknowledges the truth' (Ch. 5:9).

Let us sum up in the words of the prophet Jeremiah the true voice of wisdom. 'Thus says the Lord: Let not the wise man glory in his wisdom, neither let the mighty man glory in his might, let not the rich man glory in his riches, but let him glory in this, that he understands and knows Me, that I am the Lord who exercises lovingkindness, judgement and righteousness in the earth, for in these things I delight, says the Lord' (9: 22, 23).

40

Va'etchanan
COVENANT BETWEEN GOD AND ISRAEL

And the Lord said to Moses: 'Write down these words, for yourself, for according to these words have I sealed a covenant with you and Israel.'

Exodus 34:27

The Lord our God made a covenant with us in Horev. The Lord made this covenant not with our fathers alone, but with us, even us, who are all of us alive this day.

Deuteronomy 5:2, 3

A COVENANT in the Bible is generally a binding oath between two parties. The Hebrew name for it is '*brit*' and constitutes a mutual agreement between individuals. Sometimes the covenant is accompanied by an external sign, such as circumcision, and the observance of the Shabbat. The perpetual covenant God has with the Jewish people is the highest form of relationship; for it is based on Israel's pledge to live in accordance with the commandments and God's love for us, as it says: 'And who is like Your people Israel, a nation one in the earth' (1 Chronicles 17:21).

In this week's parashah, Moses expresses this idea to a generation about to enter the Promised Land. He reminds them of the special mutual relationship that exists between God and Israel, when at Mount Sinai all the tribes of Israel pledged their allegiance to God. Later in the prophetic books, especially in Hosea, Jeremiah and Ezekiel, this concept of love is symbolically expressed by referring to this relationship as one of love between husband and wife.

This covenant relationship is based on recognising the Torah as God's words and the need to study and fulfil the laws. Moses reminds the people: 'Now, O Israel, listen to the decrees and the ordinances that I teach you to perform ... you shall not add to the word that I command you, nor shall you subtract from it, to observe the commandments of the Lord your God' (Deuteronomy 4:1, 2). Such importance did our Sages attach to the value of the Torah as the living word of God, that the Gemara in Shabbat states that the heavenly angels objected to it being given to mortals. Moses, however, proved to them through arguments that man was sufficiently deserving to receive the Torah (88b).

In another aggadic teaching about Israel's acceptance of the Torah, Rabbi Shmuel bar Nachmani asked: 'What is the meaning of the passage: "You have captured My heart, My sister, O bride; You have captured My heart with one eye" (Song of Songs 4:9) At first when you accepted the Torah, you (Israel) attracted Me only with your mind (one eye), but after you carried out by practising its teachings you saw its physical value as well (two eyes)' (ibid.).

Again, in another homiletical exposition the Tanna Rabbi Elazar taught: 'But for the Torah heaven and earth would not endure, for it is said: "If not for my covenant by day and night, I had not have set up the laws of heaven and earth"' (Jeremiah 33:25) (Pesachim 65).

To study the Torah was to be the duty of every Jew and it was necessary for one to be as close as possible to a Torah environment. Thus, the advice of Rabbi Nehorai who said: 'Go as a voluntary exile to a place of Torah, and do not assume that it will come after you, for your fellow students will ensure that it will remain with you' (Avot 4:19).

Throughout Jewish history, it was the Torah which preserved Israel in their dispersion. The Sages asked: 'How did Israel survive when in Galut, and their precious gifts and possessions taken away from them?' The Midrash answers: 'It was the scroll of the Torah, and its study day and night, that preserved its national integrity' (Sifra Bechukotai). The following story illustrates this. Rabbi Yosi ben Kisma said: 'Once I was walking along the road when a man met and greeted me, and I returned his greeting. He said to me: "Rabbi, if you are willing to live with us in our place I will give you a million gold dinars, as well as precious stones and pearls." I replied: "Were you to give me all the silver and gold and precious stones and pearls in the world I would not live anywhere except in a place of Torah"' (Ethics of the Fathers 6:9).

The complementary ideals of study and practice of Torah and Mitzvah were the ingredients of the Jewish way of life. They were the ideals which needed constant attention and no matter how much Torah a Jew studied there were no ends to acquiring Torah knowledge. Indeed. no matter how much knowledge one acquires in studying the Bible, Talmud and other sources of Rabbinic literature, one knows just 'a little'. In the words of Ben Bag-Bag: 'Turn it over (the Torah), and turn it over, for everything is in it. And look into it, and become grey and old therein, and do not stir from it, for you have no better portion than this' (ibid. 5:25).

41

Ekev (1)

RECOGNISING GOD'S GREATNESS

And he afflicted you and suffered you to hunger and fed you with manna
... that He might make you know that man does not live
by bread alone but by everything that proceeds
out of the mouth of the Lord does man live.

Deuteronomy 8:3

You shall fear the Lord your God; Him shall you serve; and to Him
shall you cleave, and by His name shall you swear.

Deuteronomy 10:20

BEFORE taking leave of the Jewish people, Moses calls upon them not to forget God either in times of adversity or in prosperity. Just as the manna in the wilderness was a constant trial to test their faith in God so also in times of success and prosperity they were not to forget the goodness and blessings of God who is the source of all blessings

Moses, in appealing to the nation, calls upon them to recognise and appreciate the good things that are provided for them. The fruits of man's work, of his creativity and success, were to be enjoyed, and there was nothing wrong in benefiting and finding happiness in one's lot. However, in order that we recognise and express our gratitude to God that 'He brought us out of Egypt' and that 'the entire earth is His' (Exodus 19:5), the Sages instituted a series of blessings to be recited on different occasions. In Gemara Berachot, it is stated: 'Whoever enjoys any worldly pleasure without reciting a benediction to God is guilty of committing a theft' (ibid. 35a).

The Men of the Great Assembly – '*Anshei Knesset Hagedolah*' – in the time of Ezra the Scribe and other members of this august body thus established the formulae to be recited on various occasions. Based on the command 'the earth is Mine' they established, for example, that every meal at which bread was eaten, was to be followed by Grace after Meals. They further ruled that prayers be recited daily in the morning, afternoon and evening and that most mitzvot require a blessing prior to their performance. Basically, they could be divided into three groups. First, blessings offered in gratitude for the pleasures one derives from eating, drinking and other forms of enjoyment. Second, blessings of praise and thanksgiving recited in the early part of the morning service. Third, blessings on the performance of mitzvot.

In Gemara Sotah on the text: 'And Abraham proclaimed the Name of the Lord' (Genesis 21:33) Resh Lakish said: 'Read not "and he called" but "he made to call"', thereby teaching that our father Abraham caused the Name of the Holy One, blessed be He, to be familiar in the mouths of others. How did he do this? After his guests ate and drank, they stood up to bless him. But he would say to them: "Did you eat of my food? You ate of the food which belongs to God of the Universe, thank, praise and bless Him who spoke and the world was created" (10b). In this manner did Abraham draw people closer to God in recognising Him as the source of all blessings.

This is the task of everyone like Abraham in sanctifying the Name of God and being a witness to His existence and creation. The Talmud elaborates on this by asking: 'How does one love the Lord your God? – by making His Name beloved through you. If one studies scriptures and the Oral Law, speaks kindly to his fellow man, is honest and honourable in his dealings, to such a one the Bible states: "You are My servant, in whom I will be glorified"' (Isaiah 49:3) (Yoma 86a).

In the tumult of life's sufferings, one may often forget the thought of the One and only God. But when we say: 'Blessed are You, O Lord', we recognise and appreciate His infinite goodness and wish to cleave to Him by directing our life directly under His care. King David, who was wise and pious, reflecting on his attachment to God, framed his love by stating in the Book of Psalms: 'Bless the Lord, O my soul, and do not forget all His kindnesses' (103:2). Yes, to strive and cleave to God is the closest one can get in our relationship of service to Him.

42

Ekev (2)

CLEAVING TO GOD

You shall fear the Lord your God; Him shall you serve; and to Him
shall you cleave, and by His name shall you swear.

Deuteronomy 10:20

ON NUMEROUS occasions, the Torah calls upon Israel not to forget, particularly in the days of prosperity, God's goodness. Later in the parsha this warning is brought home in the form of changes that confront man in the days of prosperity. 'Beware lest you forget the Lord your God ... when you have eaten and are satisfied, and have built good houses, and dwell therein, and when your flocks multiply, and your silver and your gold is multiplied' (ibid. 8:11–13).

It is a common human error for man to detest the guiding hand of Divine Providence in times of distress and misfortune yet he fails to recognise God's goodness in days of prosperity. The real test comes when, in times of plenty and power, one should remember that 'it is He who gives one power to get wealth' (ibid. 18).

Moses, in his appeal to the nation, reminds them of the consequences of forgetting God and the rich reward that awaits those who recognise and are obedient to His will. The Sages were ever mindful that the natural plenitude and the fruits of man's work, of his creativity and success, were to be enjoyed and that there was nothing wrong in benefitting and finding blessing in them. However, as '*li kol ha'aretz*' (for all the earth is Mine) (Exodus 19:5) and as God is the creator of all things, it was constantly incumbent upon man to remember his duty to serve Him by observing His commandments, judgments and statutes.

The Gemara in Berachot enquires: 'Where do we find that reciting grace after meals is ordained in the Torah? Because it says: "And you shall eat and be satisfied and bless"' (21a). Our Rabbis, therefore, said:

'Whoever enjoys any worldly pleasure without offering a benediction is guilty of theft from that which belongs to God' (ibid. 35a). Life provides us with numerous benefits and enjoyments. The *Anshei Knesset Hagedolah* (men of the Great Assembly), the spiritual leaders in the time of Ezra the Scribe, established the formulae of all the blessings to be pronounced on various occasions. One was not permitted to change, add or subtract from them and anyone who deviated from the form which they laid down falls into error.

In addition to the three daily services, one recites daily, there are three other benedictions that they instituted. They are: 1. Blessings to be said in gratitude for the pleasures one derives from eating, drinking and scenting, known as Blessings of Enjoyment. 2. Blessings on the performance of religious duties, known as Blessings of the Performance of Mitzvot. 3. Blessings of Peratiyut – these are blessings of thanksgiving and praise recited in the early part of the Morning Service and in the Amidah. By means of these three benedictions, the Jew acknowledges his dependence on God at all times. Furthermore, included in these blessings are those which affect one on every possible occasion; from witnessing lightning, thunderstorms, hearing good news, buying a new home, to recovery from illness and a father's blessing on his son reaching bar mitzvah, when he can distinguish between right and wrong, and become an adult member of the community. Furthermore, it is meritorious to pray in the synagogue in congregational prayer, for as a spiritual centre praying with our fellow men makes us united and inspires loyalty.

In Gemara Sotah, commenting on the text: 'And Abraham proclaimed the Name of the Lord' (Genesis 21:33) the Sages say the words 'and he proclaimed' to mean 'he caused God's Name to be familiar in the mouths of others'. How did he do this? After his guests ate and drank in his home, they stood to bless him. But he would say to them: 'Did you eat my food? You ate of the food which belongs to the God of the Universe. Therefore then, praise and bless Him who spoke and created the world' (10b). The goal to strive after God in love, in deed and in action is best reflected in our blessings to others. In the Gemara Rabbi Hama asked: 'What is the meaning of the text: "You shall walk after the Lord our God" (Deuteronomy 13:5)? Is it possible for a human being to walk after the Shechinah – Divine Presence? But the meaning is to walk in the attributes of God' (Sotah 14a). The purpose of life is to imitate God in action. As God is merciful, so we are to be merciful. As He loves and cares for His creatures, so you also love all His creatures. As He is gracious, so you also be gracious. As He is long-suffering, so you also show yourself long-suffering. As he is rich in love and merciful, so should you be not poor in love and mercy. As He forgives, so you, too, forgive. Thus God shows us the way to draw close to Him. It is through our actions and conduct towards our fellow men that we can understand and cleave to Him.

Tradition has it that King David, who was wise and pious, reflecting on his nearness to God, best framed this love by stating: 'Bless the Lord, O my soul, and do not forget all His benefits' (Psalm 103:2). Indeed, striving to recognise and appreciate God's infinite goodness is perhaps the closest one can get to cleaving to God and living a life directly under His care.

43

Re'eh

PRIEST, PROPHET AND SAGE

Happy is the man that findeth wisdom, and the man that obtaineth understanding. For its merchandise is better than the commerce of silver, and the gain thereof than fine gold.

Proverbs 3:13

ON A NUMBER of occasions, Moses, the prophet and lawgiver, calls on the Jewish people to study and understand the wisdom of the Torah. In Sefer Devarim, he says: 'For this is your wisdom and understanding in the sight of the people' (Deuteronomy 4:6). Again, 'See I have set before you today a blessing and a curse. The blessing if you shall hearken to the commandments of the Lord your God' (ibid. 11:26–27). King Solomon again informs us: 'How much better to get wisdom than gold. Yes, to get understanding is rather to be chosen than silver' (Proverbs 16:16).

Wisdom is a divine gift which gives both grace and power to man. Perhaps the fittest definition of a wise man has been provided by the Tanna Ben Zoma, who asked: 'Who is wise?' And he answered: 'He who learns from all.' (Ethics of the Fathers 4:1) Man's real wealth lies in his store of knowledge and it was King Solomon, the wisest of all men, who in his prayer to God requested wisdom above other material values. 'Grant your servant an understanding heart, to judge your people, to distinguish between good and evil.' (I Kings, 3:9) Solomon's wisdom is the subject of many Rabbinic legends and as expressed by our Sages he unravelled the mysteries of the world, solved difficult riddles and even understood the language of birds and beasts.

In biblical times, there were three classes of teachers – the priests, the prophets and the wise. The priest had the duty of providing the community with instruction in the practices of religion as expressed by the prophet Malachi: 'For the lips of the Cohen should safeguard knowledge, and people should seek teaching from his mouth, for he is the agent of God, Master of Legions' (2:7). It was the priests' responsibility, in addition to their special task in the Temple services, to make the nation adhere to the Torah laws which regulated their daily worship.

The prophet, on the other hand, spoke in the name of God. As God's spokesman he was endowed with the divine gift of both receiving and imparting the message and was chosen often against his own will to convey as God's spokesman the divine word regardless of whether or not the people wished to hear it (see Ezekiel 3:11).

Whilst the priests and prophets acted and spoke with divine authority, the wise taught what they believed to be true and right. They never presumed to say: 'Thus saith the Lord', but were earnest seekers of the good life, wishing to instruct others in how to attain true wisdom. As there was a literature of priests and prophets, so we find there emerged a literature of these wise Sages known under the general title of 'Wisdom Literature'.

The following books are incorporated in the Hebrew scriptures: Proverbs, Psalms, Job and Ecclesiastes, and they reflect the concept of wisdom as developed in the long course of Israel's religious history. Biblical wisdom was a way of life, an attitude of thinking that emphasised the well-being of the individual and his social relationships. The wisdom teachers, or Hachamim, sought to provide rules and examples of personal morals to their pupils to enable them to avoid the pitfalls that would face them in life.

In the Book of Proverbs, for example, the purpose of this work is to bring home the importance of attaining understanding which will lead to the true knowledge of God. It was to make a person aware of what was expected of him and what was the purpose of his existence. Time and time again, the instructor advises on the importance of wisdom and the dire consequences if one were to ignore his guidance. In his personification of wisdom, he says: 'Because I have called out, and you refused, I have stretched out my hand, and no man responded ... I also in your calamity will laugh ... for they hated knowledge, and did not choose the fear of the Lord; they would none of my counsel, they despised my reproof' (ibid. 1:24–30). Again it is stated: 'Wisdom cries out aloud in the streets, raises her voice in the squares ... How long will you simple ones love simplicity ... you dullards hate knowledge?' (ibid. 1:21–22). In chapter 2, the preacher calls again: 'If you make your ear attentive to wisdom and your mind open to discernment ... if you seek it as you do silver and search for it as for treasures, then you will understand the fear of the Lord and attain knowledge of God' (2–5).

As one of the Wisdom books, the preacher brings home the importance of seeking knowledge and the need to safeguard oneself from the dangers and pitfalls that particularly surround the ignorant.

We see that Wisdom, in these books, is not viewed as a natural gift but something that needed to be learnt, and as it was a divine gift, it offered reward to those who were willing to submit to its teaching.

In the Book of Job, the author offers the definition of a wise man. Let us quote his words: 'But wisdom, where shall it be found, and where is the place of understanding? ... It cannot be gotten for gold, neither shall silver be weighed for the price thereof ... Behold, the fear of the Lord that is wisdom; and to depart from evil is understanding' (Job 28:12–28).

Interestingly, it is Job himself who, faced with a series of calamites including bodily suffering, claims by his limited knowledge to question God's decree on him. In a series of encounters with his three friends Eliphaz, Bildad and Zopher, he questions God's judgment arguing his innocence and righteousness. Throughout the dialogue he asserts his piety and goodness and is prepared to argue his case. Towards the end of the Book, God speaks to Job saying: 'Who is this ... who speaks without knowledge? Where were you when I laid the foundations of the earth? Have you ever commanded the day ... or penetrated the vaults of snow? ... Can you send up an order to the clouds? ... Is it by your wisdom that the hawk grows pinions? Can one who should be disciplined complain against the Lord?' (ibid. 38 ff.).

On hearing of God's great works in creation and His continued providence, Job finally gives way. He says: 'See, I am of small worth, what can I answer you? ... I have spoken once and will not reply twice ... I know you can do everything. Nothing you propose is impossible for you ... Indeed, I have spoken without knowledge of things beyond me, things which I did not know ... Therefore, I recant and relent, being but dust and ashes' (ibid. 40:2–6).

At the end of Ecclesiastes, King Solomon speaking of man's nature realises the limits of human knowledge and sums up man's task in life. 'The essence of the matter, when all is considered: Fear God and keep his commandments, for this is man's whole duty. The fear of the Lord is the beginning and end of all wisdom; for this is the true goal of one's existence' (ibid. 12: 13, 14).

44

Shoftim

ETHICS

*And the Levites ... and the stranger, and the fatherless,
and the widow, that are within your gates
shall come and eat and be satisfied.*

Deuteronomy 14:29

THE AIM of Judaism throughout the Bible is to establish a relationship between man and God. Vital though this concept may be, it also, in addition, seeks to establish a just and humane relationship between man and his neighbour. Throughout the scriptures, the Torah deals directly or indirectly with human conduct and calls upon us time and again, in the words of the prophet Isaiah: 'Learn to do good; seek justice and relieve the oppressed' (1:17). The following passage in the Talmud expresses this idea: 'One who devotes himself to the mere study of the Torah without engaging in works of mercy and love, is like one who has no God' (Avodah Zarah 17b).

Man who is created in the image of God must endeavour to model his life after the ways of God. Explaining the verse: 'You shall be holy; for I the Lord your God am holy' (Leviticus 19:2), the Sages teach: 'As I am gracious, so be you gracious, as I am merciful, so be you merciful, as I am holy, so be you holy' (Sotah 14a).

The basis of human ethics is of paramount importance as laid down in the text: 'You shall love your neighbour as yourself' (Leviticus 19:18) and the attainment of godliness to be attained through human relationship is essential in man's relationship with God. It has been said that Judaism is a religion of justice rather than love. While it is true that justice is one of the three pillars of Judaism, as stated: 'On three things the world stands – on truth, justice and peace' (Pirke Avot 1:18), yet Judaism is no less a religion of love than it is of justice.

In Chapter 19 of Leviticus, loving one's neighbour as oneself is of special significance, for it might relate to one with whom one has no blood relationship, or indeed to someone whom one may not even know. Yet we are told to love our neighbour as we love ourselves.

There are a number of instances mentioned in the Bible which express our relationship with others. 'If there be among you a needy man, one of your brethren, within any of your gates ... you shall not harden your heart, nor shut your hand from your needy brother; but you shall surely open your hand to him' (Deuteronomy 15:7,8). Again, the ethics of love demand that care be shown to the defenceless and weak, the widow and the fatherless. 'If you lend money to any of My people, even to the poor with you, you shall not be to him as a creditor; neither shall you lay upon him interest' (Exodus 22:24).

Compare these teachings towards the stranger, foreigner and needy with those of ancient Egypt, Babylon, Greece or Rome, who considered all outsiders as barbarians and amongst whom the strong would despoil the weak. Perhaps the view of Judaism was best expressed by the renowned Hillel who rephrased the law of 'love your neighbour as yourself' with 'What is hateful to you, do not to your neighbour' (Shabbat 31a). This, declared Hillel, is the fundamental principle of the Torah, the remainder being but a commentary. Indeed, this rule of conduct is the essence of our faith and applicable to all people.

In dealing with one's relationship with others, it is important to consider how our Sages in the Talmud dealt with verbal promises and with property transactions. Commenting on the text: 'Just balances, just weights, a just ephah and a just hin, shall you have' (Leviticus 19:36), Rabbi Jose, son of Rabbi Judah, said: 'From this we learn that a man must not speak one thing with his mouth and another with his heart.' (Baba Metzia 49a) Rabbi Yohanan further taught that if a person promised to give another a gift and later retracted it, this would be considered a breach of faith.

The highest degree of ethical conduct is when one abides by and honours his word in matters of transactions. Whilst legally every transaction, in order to become valid, requires a formal mode of acquisition, known as a 'kinyan', yet in matters of buying and selling, one who reneges on a verbal agreement is called a '*mechusar emunah*' (one who is lacking faith).

So much emphasis did the Rabbis place on the spoken word that they not only stated that the retractor lacked a sense of honesty but scathingly said: 'He who exacted punishment from the generation of the Flood (Genesis 6:13) and the generation of the Dispersion (ibid. 11:9) will also exact punishment from one who does not abide by his word' (Mishna Baba Metzia 4:2). From this, it is vital to understand how deeply our Sages were concerned with the sacredness of the spoken word, in dealing with 'loving one's neighbour as oneself'. Indeed the essence of religion is our relationship with others and that our 'yes' should be a 'yes' in our rule of conduct.

45

Ki Thetze

THE ETERNAL MESSAGE

Remember what Amalek did to you when you were leaving Egypt ... that he struck down those of you who were hindmost, all the weaklings at your rear when you were faint and exhausted ... You shall not forget.

Deuteronomy 25:17–19

IN ADDITION to this morning's parsha, we read on the Sabbath before Purim – called '*Shabbat Zachor*' – of the cowardly and treacherous attack by Amalek on the weak and feeble when the Israelites left Egypt. The command to remember this unprovoked attack finds its connection to the story of Purim when Haman, a descendant of Agag, king of Amalek, wished to exterminate all Jews throughout the Persian kingdom. However, his evil designs were unsuccessful and ended with Haman being hanged, the decree of destruction being annulled and the victory of the Jews over their enemies.

Haman came to be regarded as the prototype of the arch-enemy of Jews throughout the ages. By nature, Jews are not vindictive or vengeful. If anything, we are distinguished as the one oppressed and compassionate, not just to our fellow men but also to animals. So it does seem strange that we are commanded 'to blot out the memory of Amalek from under the heaven – you shall not forget'.

History has shown us that, from time immemorial, many nations have tried various means to wipe us off the face of the earth. But even in the case of the Egyptians who tried various ways to oppress and destroy Israel, the Torah states: 'You shall not abhor an Egyptian because you were a sojourner in his land' (Deuteronomy 23:8).

So what was Amalek's crime, that we are commanded not to forget its treachery? Why must we recall this evil deed continuously? The answer is offered by the Torah itself. 'How they met you on the way and smote the hindmost of you, all that was weak at your rear, when you were faint and exhausted, and he feared not God.' Amalek had no reason to attack the Israelites. They did not present any danger or threat. Amalek had heard of the miracles performed by God which led to the exodus from Egypt, yet they attacked without any provocation from Israel. There was no justification for this inhuman attack except that they feared not God. The Egyptians, on the other hand, may have considered that the Israelites had greatly multiplied during their stay in Egypt and might be a threat and join forces with others if the country were invaded.

When we consider Jewish history, we realise that there is no other nation which has experienced a past like ours. Commenc-ing with the birth of Abraham up until the present day, Jews have been faced with suffering, persecution and oppression. With the destruction of both Temples, we lost our autonomy and have wandered from one country to another seeking refuge.

Shabbat Zachor reminds us of our arch-enemies. It was such events as the Crusades, pogroms, the Inquisition and in our time the Holocaust that we recall today and say 'Remember – do not forget.'

Indeed, unlike the story of Purim when Haman's evil plan to exterminate our people became known to Mordecai, queen Esther and the Jews, in the case of the Holocaust most Jews were unaware of Hitler's plan for our mass extinction. Aubrey Hersh writes: 'The Germans mounted the greatest deception of all times to allay the fears of the Jews until the last moment, talking of resettlement but never of mass murder, gas chambers or death camps.'

Seventy years ago, six million of our people, men, women and children, died for no other reason than that they were Jews. In the history of the human race, there has never been anything like this before and we pray there will never be anything like this again.

The story of Amalek and his successors – such as Haman and the Holocaust perpetrators – calls upon each one of us to recall their evil deeds and ensure that it never be forgotten. Those who committed such evils believed in power over justice, might against right, fascism as opposed to the sanctity of human life. We can only overcome those who wish to perpetuate such evil by constant vigilance and by holding aloft the ideals of the Torah where morality, justice, love and brotherhood are part of our lives.

46

Ki Thavo

JOY

And you shall take for yourselves on the first day the fruit of a citron tree, the branches of date palms, twigs of a plaited tree, and brook willows; and you shall rejoice before the Lord your God for seven days.

Leviticus 23:40

THE FESTIVAL of Sukkot is an eternal reminder of how our ancestors wandered for forty years in a wilderness. During those years they survived the long journeys by their faith in divine protection. The temporary booths, flimsily constructed, could never have afforded safety but for God's protective arm.

The Bible also refers to this festival as '*Chag Ha'asif*' (the feast of ingathering) when the people, having gathered in their crops, rejoiced before the Lord in gratitude for the blessings He bestowed upon them. The agricultural character of this festival received symbolic expression through the use of '*Arba Minim*' (the four species) enumerated in our opening verse.

The third name given to this festival is '*chag*' (feast) – 'you shall celebrate it as a festival for the Lord seven days'. The ceremony which created the greatest enthusiasm for this festival was 'the ceremony of water drawing' when the Temple existed. So great was the rejoicing that our Rabbis stated: 'He who has not witnessed the joy around "*Bet Hashoeva*" (Ceremony of the Water Drawing') has not witnessed true rejoicing in his life' (Talmud Sukkah 51a). Details of this ceremony are described in the Mishna Sukkot, chapter 5, where a full account of the festival is given which lasted for six nights.

The need to be joyful was not to be restricted just to festive occasions. The Torah commands us in a number of places to be happy. 'And you shall rejoice in all the good which the Lord your God has given you' (Deuteronomy 26:11). 'Serve the Lord with gladness, come

139

before His presence with singing' (Psalms 100:2). 'Be glad and rejoice for the Lord had done great things' (Joel 2:21).

Dealing with the *'Tochacha'* (Warnings) at the end of Deuteronomy, the Torah describes God's anger against the House of Israel for not serving God with gladness of heart: 'Because you did not serve the Lord, your God, with gladness and goodness of heart' (28:46). We thus see that joy and happiness is considered an important part in our service to God and that His anger is aroused when we fail to do so.

The Gemara in Sanhedrin 94a states that the Almighty wished to appoint King Hezekiah as the Messiah but the attribute of Justice argued that as the King did not offer up song and praise to God for all the miracles which He performed for him he should not be appointed for this role.

Whilst it is true that following the destruction of the Second Temple and the disasters that followed, the Sages were opposed to the excesses of human joy, yet refraining from legitimate pleasure was considered a sin similar to that of the Nazirite who had to bring an atoning sacrifice at the end of his Naziriteship for denying himself the permissible pleasures of life (see Midrash Sifre Numbers 30).

The greatest source of joy was the performance of the mitzvoth *'simcha shel mitzvah'*. King David saw the divine commandments as a source of joy by stating: 'The statutes of the Lord are right, rejoicing the heart' (Psalms 19:8). The joy that should accompany the fulfilment of a precept is illustrated in the Gemara by the following account. 'Rabbi Eleazar ben Zadok said: This was the custom of the people of Jerusalem. When a man left his house, he carried his *"lulav"* (palm branch) in his hand, went to the synagogue with the *"lulav"* in his hand, recited the Shema and his prayers, read the Torah, at all times with the *"lulav"* in his hand. When he went to visit the sick or comfort the mourner, he would go with the *"lulav"* in his hand, to show how much joy they had in performing a religious duty' (Talmud Sukkah 41).

In the Book of Psalms there are many verses of praise and song which express the need to be joyous in serving the Lord. Rabbi Ibbu explained the verse: 'But let the righteous be glad, let them exalt before God; yes, let them rejoice with gladness' (Ps. 68:4) as follows: 'When you stand to pray, you have to be glad that you are praying to God, who is the Creator of the Universe' (Midrash Shoher Tov). Similarly, there is no greater joy than that of fulfilling a precept. Indeed, divine worship and fulfilment of the mitzvot performed in joy offer us a spiritual uplift and ways of serving God.

Moreover, the need to be aware of God's goodness to us should help to keep us in a state of joy and happiness. It would make us aware that though life is short and unpredictable, the element of joy even in our ordinary daily life is a means of our service to God. Indeed, the duty to serve God with gladness is the whole purpose of life and happy is the one who attains it.

47

Nitzavim

THE TRUE LEADER

*And I call heaven and earth to witness against you this day that I have set
before you life and death, the blessing and the curse; therefore choose life
that you and your seed may live.*

Deuteronomy 30:19

THE END of Moses' life and leadership was approaching. He was
told by God that he was not destined to bring the Israelites into
Canaan but to ascend Mt. Abarim where he would see the land
before he died. During the forty years in the wilderness he had served
the nation well. When they had left Egypt they were a disorganised
group but under his leadership he had united them as one people.

The Bible informs us that 'there had not risen a prophet since in
Israel like unto Moses' (ibid. 34:10) whose pre-eminence is one of the
Thirteen Principles of Moses Maimonides' Faith. What, indeed, made
Moses such a great prophet and leader? Amongst his many gifts and his
towering character, in what lay that greatness that singled him out as a
true leader?

Amongst his many qualities, there are two that show us the type of
leader he was. The first was that on being told that he was not destined
to lead the Israelites across the Jordan he focused on appointing a
successor who had the moral and spiritual strength to bring the people
on the final stage of their journey to their homeland. Accordingly, he
asked God: 'Let the Lord, the God of all spirits, set a man over the
congregation' (Numbers 27:16). The Midrash, commenting on the
phrase 'God of all spirits', explains Moses' request. Moses said:
'Sovereign of the Universe, You know the minds of all men and how
the mind of one differs from that of another. Grant them a leader who
will be able to bear with the different minds of your children.' The Bnei
Yisrael were not an easy people to lead. They were stubborn and prone

to complain. To lead such a people demanded a spirit, one that was not to be easily swayed by the many conflicting and divisive opinions among them. He had not to be autocratic but had to take the initiative at all times and show strength of character by firm and decisive action.

God responded to Moses' request. He told him that there was one person who was qualified for this undertaking – Joshua, the son of Nun. Joshua had the necessary qualities and it was to Moses' credit that Joshua was the right person to succeed him.

The second great quality that Moses possessed was his ability to foresee the future. It was at the foot of Mount Sinai that Israel became an '*am segulah*'. There they were granted the Torah, a covenant by which the nation was united in allegiance to one God. Through the acceptance of the Torah, Israel was to be a 'kingdom of priests and a holy nation'. Throughout his leadership, Moses taught them the importance of the laws of the Torah as a 'tree of life'.

But what about the future? Before his death, he reminded them that they were a small nation in number, smaller than other nations. But how would they survive among people more numerous and more powerful than they were? How would they be able to withstand the immoral practices of the nations in whose midst they would dwell in the future? The answer, he says, lay in their observance of the Torah. As long as Israel studied and kept the Torah, they would be able to survive. As long as Israel observed the words of the Covenant, even in exile, they would be able to withstand the challenges of life.

This was the message that Moses, as leader, felt it necessary to stress. Like a beacon of light, like a faithful watchman, Moses mapped out the path by which Israel would continue. Indeed, the preservation of our nation throughout our wanderings and exile has been due to the fact that we kept alive the teachings of the Torah. This was the lesson that Moses as leader left with us. 'I have set before you life and death, the blessing and the curse, therefore choose life, that you may live, you and your seed'.

48

Vayyelech
DESTINY OF MAN

For I have kept the ways of the Lord, and have not wickedly departed from my God. For all His ordinances were before me.

Samuel II, 22:22,23

A S WE APPROACH the New Year, the Day of Judgment, we believe that life has meaning and turn to our Creator in prayer 'to inscribe us in the Book of Life'. But the question we ask ourselves is: What is man? What is the purpose and destiny of life? According to Jewish teaching, man is not a tool but an essential part of the universe. The Zohar refers to him as 'Monarch of the world'. The Psalmist confirms this view, for it asks: 'What is frail man that You should be mindful of him? Yet, You have made him slightly lower than the angels, and crowned him with soul and splendour. You have given him dominion over Your handiwork. You have placed everything under his feet' (8:5–7).

Man, endowed with reason, has the ability to master nature's resources and, as it were, is God's ambassador. But the question we still ask: what difference does it make how we define man? Why speculate as to his essence and role in life? The answer is that it makes a great difference whether he considers himself as striving to become king and master or as a meaningless player in the course of life. If he sees his existence as little lower than the angels, then he will strive to live morally and become angelic and not a slave working without any meaningful goal. One hears the arguments put forward by the perpetrators of the most heinous crimes committed against humanity. When asked to explain the inhuman and brutal torture of other humans and how they could stoop to such evil, the response given was: 'We were merely carrying out orders'.

Let us consider how Jewish law regards the taking of human life. In Judaism, murder was considered the worst criminal act and the most

144

sacrilegious. Suppose a king or one in authority, under the threat of death, ordered one to commit murder: Jewish law says: '*Yehoreg ve'al ya'avor*' (Let him die and not transgress). Maimonides points out that no human being has the right to pardon a murderer for this most terrible act. He writes: 'The courts are warned against the acceptance of ransom from the murderer, even if he is ready to pay all the money in the world and even if the avenger of blood agrees to set the murderer free. For the life of the murdered person is not the possession of the avenger of blood, but the possession of the Holy One, blessed be He' (Laws of Murder 1:4).

In Pirke Avot, Rabbi Akiva said: 'Beloved is man for he was made in the image of God; still greater was the love that it was made known to him that he was created in the image of God' (3:14). Simon ben Azzai went even further than this by saying that 'man made in the image of God' was more important than the Biblical command to 'love one's neighbour'.

The sacredness of every human life is well illustrated in the following Mishnah. 'If heathens say to a group of women: "Give us one of you that we may defile her and if not we will defile all of you" they should all suffer defilement, rather than surrender a single soul' (Terumot 8:12). We thus see the importance the Rabbis placed on the value of human life.

Let us conclude with the following Biblical story. The Patriarch Abraham is informed by God that He is about to destroy the wicked people of Sodom. On hearing this, Abraham pleads on their behalf. On learning that there are not fifty righteous men there, he continues to plead on behalf of forty, thirty, twenty and ten in the hope that the people might be spared (Genesis: 18:23–32).

In his intercession for the wicked people of Sodom, Abraham shows not just the nobility of his character but his concern that human beings were about to die and his desire that they should be pardoned.

The sacredness of the human personality is perhaps best described in the Mishna 'God created a single man only to teach that if anyone destroy a single soul from the children of men, Scripture charges him as though he had destroyed a whole world, and whoever serves the life of a single soul, Scripture credits him as though he had saved a whole world' (Sanhedrin 4:5).

49

Ha'azinu

GRATITUDE

And David spoke to the Lord the words of this song in the day that the
Lord delivered him out of the hand of all his enemies
and out of the hand of Saul.

2 Samuel 22:1

I N THIS SONG, King David offers his thanks to God for delivering him
from his enemies. He traces the hand of Divine Providence in
protecting him in the events that occurred in his life and his gratitude
for the mercies bestowed upon him.

Similarly, one reads of the song Moses composed at the Red Sea
when all Israel perceived the hand of God delivering them from the
Egyptian army. 'Then sang Moses and the children of Israel this song to
the Lord' (Exodus 15:1). At this moment of thanksgiving both Moses
and Israel sang together. The Gemara in Sotah states: 'Moses sang one
verse and the people repeated after him all that he said' (30b). In other
words, there was a decorum unique among the entire Jewish people.
The great unity of thought expressed in this song was a profound
spiritual event never to be repeated in history. Our Sages regarded this
song as one of the ten songs that were ever sung from the beginning of
the creation of the world to the Messianic Era (Mechilta 15:1).

Songs and praise are the most direct way of thanking the Lord for
the mercies he bestows upon us. When the Temples existed, music and
song were ways by which the Levites would serve and considered
principal tasks in the Temple.

Hezekiah, king of Judah, was considered by the Sages to be a
completely righteous person. During his twenty-nine year reign, he
devoted himself to 'strengthening the bonds between Israel and God' by
studying the Torah. (Sanhedrin 94b; Song Rabbah 4:8). Through his
efforts, knowledge of the Torah spread throughout the land and it is

said: 'They searched from Dan to Beersheba and no-one was found to be ignorant from Gabbat to Antipatris and no boy or girl, man or woman was found who was not thoroughly versed in the laws of cleanness and uncleanness.' (ibid. 94b) Hezekiah was so righteous that when he died the Rabbis placed a Sefer Torah – Scroll of the Law – on his coffin, and declared: 'This one fulfilled all that which is written in this Scroll' (Baba Kamma 17a).

With all this we are told: 'The Holy One, blessed be He, wished to appoint King Hezekiah as the Messiah, and Sennacherib (King of Assyria and Babylonia) as Gog and Magog, whereupon the Attribute of Justice protested it before the Holy One blessed be He, Sovereign of the Universe, saying "if you did not make David the Messiah who uttered so many hymns and psalms before You, will you appoint Hezekiah as Messiah who did not sing a hymn in spite of all the miracles which You performed for him?"' (Sanhedrin 94a).

In Deuteronomy ch. 26:1–11 the Torah prescribes the details of a ritual that had to be performed by the farmer in the land of Israel: 'And it shall be when you are come into the land which the Lord your God gives you as an inheritance, and you possess it, and dwell in it, that you shall take of the first of all the fruit of the ground ... and you shall put it into a basket ... and the priest shall take the basket out of your hand ... And you shall speak ... I have brought the first of the fruit of the land which You O Lord has given me.'

This bringing of the ripened first fruits and declaration by the owner was an expression of gratitude to God for all the blessings conferred on him. Maimonides explains the reasons for this command. 'He who brings the first fruits in the basket upon his shoulders, and proclaims the kindness and goodness of God. This ceremony teaches man that it is essential in the service of God to recall previous experiences of suffering and distress in days of comfort and to acknowledge His sovereignty' (Guide for the Perplexed 3:39).

Isaac Arama, the fifteenth-century commentator on the Pentateuch, offers a similar opinion. He writes: 'The essence of acknowledging divine sovereignty lies in man's gratitude to the Creator as the source of all the good, and that man himself is no way responsible for all that he has accomplished...' This is indeed the subject of the warnings contained in Moses' address to the people in Deuteronomy 4:25 ff. They would forget God's bounty and imagine that they were the authors of all the benefits they were enjoying in the Promised Land. They were therefore bidden to perform a rite that would act as a constant reminder that 'the earth is the Lord's and the fullness thereof', that everything was a gift bestowed by Him and that He was responsible for all their prosperity. Indeed, all such offerings constituted acknowledgment of Divine overlordship (Akedat Yitzchak).

In the light of the above, it is our duty to acknowledge that every day is a gift, bestowed on us. Though one can never reciprocate God's goodness to us yet there is a special obligation upon every person to remember and acknowledge with gratitude His unending mercies.

50

Vezoth Ha-berachah
PARTNERS IN CREATION

Woe to you, O land, when your king is a child, and your princes eat in the morning! Happy are you, O land, when your king is the son of nobles and your princes eat in due season.

Ecclesiastes 10:16

OUR RABBIS inform us that God created the world from a plan and that the purpose of human creation is to understand the meaning of this plan. When man was created in the image of God, he was to rule the earth and its resources by his deeds and become God's partner in the work of creation.

At the beginning of Genesis, he was called upon 'to work and guard the Garden of Eden' (2:15) thus imposing upon him the responsibility to till the soil and explore the earth for its hidden treasures. The Midrash puts it: 'Whatever was created in the six days of creation stood in need of processing. For instance, mustard seeds must be processed and wheat must be milled' (Yalkut Shimoni).

The Creator prepared all the materials and ingredients necessary for man to work with, to continue and use for his benefit. However, when man abuses the wonders of creation entrusted to his care he destroys the very purpose of his creation.

Let us quote the Midrash again. 'When the Holy One, blessed be He, created Adam, He showed him all the trees of the Garden of Eden and said to him: "See My works, how beautiful and perfect they are for you. Take care not to ruin them."' Indeed, the material world was completed, the raw materials were there and it was a challenge to him to unearth the hidden treasures.

But man's responsibility is not only to himself but to his fellow man and he was to take his proper place in society. The Talmud, commenting on the verse: 'But when the hands of Moses became heavy, they took a stone and placed it under him' (Exodus 17:12). Did not Moses have a pillow or quilt to sit on? But these were Moses' words: 'So long as the children of Israel are suffering I shall share my grief with them' (Taanit 11).

Man's role, his rights and duties, are expressed by the renowned Torah scholar, Rabbi Samson Raphael Hirsch. He writes: 'All things are servants of God, each in its time and place, in accordance with its capacity, fulfils the word of God ... In the midst of the world full of divine glory stands man. It is inconceivable that he was born merely to receive. It is inconceivable that he has no mission to his brother who serves the Lord as well' (Horeb).

But man, with all his pre-eminence in the world, is ever aware of his frailty and mortality and the sense of responsibility lies heavily on his shoulders. So how can he shoulder this great responsibility? This is, according to the Talmud, what the ministerial angels argued when they were consulted by God as to whether man should be created. They said: 'Lord of the Universe, what are his deeds?' He answered: 'Such and such are his deeds.' When the generation of the Deluge and Confusion of Tongues became sinful, the angels turned to the Almighty, saying: 'Lord of the Universe, did not we tell you of this?' To which the Lord answered them: 'Even unto old age I am He, even to hoary hairs will I endure.' (Sanhedrin 38b).

The Almighty knows and understands human weaknesses and with all that is compassionate both to the wicked and to the righteous. He left us the process of creation and charged us to do our best to continue and complete our task by using our talents in a positive manner.

Each person as an individual has the power to choose and influence society in a positive or negative way but the challenge we take in life is to do our best in being partners with God in the act of creation.

The fact that the Talmud, quoted above, states the dilemma of man's creation shows that God had faith in man's potential to do good. Yes, man falters and rebels, yet the Almighty never gives up and hopes for the best from humanity. It is this faith in us that overcame the dilemma facing God over man's creation: but it was also the belief that man can rise and live up to his potential that makes him worthy to be created in the image of God.

PART II

51

The Ten Commandments
MIDRASHIC INSIGHTS

BEFORE discussing the Ten Commandments, we need to know what is 'Midrash'. Generally, it does not deal with Halachah i.e. laws and regulations. The Sages, through parables, allegories, metaphors and maxims, wished to touch the heart of people and awaken their knowledge of God and the chosen role of Israel.

The day of the Revelation (when God's Presence descended upon Mount Sinai) and the giving of the Torah are the most remarkable events in the history of Israel and mankind. The display of thunder, lightning and blasts of the shofar announcing the Divine declaration of the Ten Commandments gave birth to the moral, educational and spiritual life of humanity and Judaism in particular. Divided into two Tablets, one dealing with our duties to God – *bein adam lemakom* – and the other with our duties to our fellow men – *bein adam lechavero* – it was a sublime summary of the fundamental teachings of Judaism.

In Midrashic literature, our Rabbis offered many homiletic commentaries through the means of Aggadah and allegorical exposition. By such means, the teachers of Talmud and Midrash brought home and emphasised the eternal significance of the Revelation at Sinai. They even went further by means of metaphor and Rabbinic legend to say that the Divine voice divided itself into seventy tongues spoken in the world so that everyone might understand its all-embracing message.

So let us begin by reviewing some of their teachings. The Torah states in Exodus 32:16 that 'the two Tablets were the work of God and the writings were the writings of God'. One chapter earlier it states again 'They were written with God's finger' (ibid. 31:18). The Gemara in Shabbat asks: Why does the Torah need to repeat twice 'it was written by God'? And the answer given is: there were two miracles associated with the writings – one that the writing could be read on both sides, meaning that the writing went completely through the Tablets from one side to the other and appeared to be written as it were on both sides in the proper order. The second miracle was that the final letter '*mem*' and the letter '*samech*' would normally have fallen out, being engraved on four sides, as there was nothing to hold them to the Tablets. Since they hung in mid-air and did not fall out – two great miracles – therefore the Torah states: 'the writing was the writing of God' 'and they were written with God's finger'.

Now, we are told, the Ten Commandments were written on two Tablets, five on each Tablet – to quote, 'He wrote them on two Tablets of stone' (Deuteronomy 5:19) indicating that five commandments were written on one Tablet and five commandments on the other Tablet. The order would then be as follows:

On one side	*The other side would be*
I am the Lord your God	Do not commit murder
You shall have no other God	Do not commit adultery
Do not take God's name in vain	Do not steal
Remembering the Sabbath day	Do not commit perjury
Honour your father and mother	Do not covet

The Midrash Yalkut Shimoni explains it was written in this manner so that each of the five commands on one side were written directly opposite the five commands on the other side to teach that each command complemented the other. For example, the first commandment: 'I am the Lord your God' corresponds to the sixth commandment 'Do not commit murder' and teaches that whoever commits murder is considered as though he denied his Creator's existence. Similarly, the eighth command 'Do not steal' corresponds to the third command – 'Do not take God's name in vain' – for whoever steals another person's money will ultimately swear falsely (see Parasha Yitro). And so on. The reason why the Sages offered this explanation was to avoid those who held that the second set of laws in the second Tablet was not as important as the first set in the first Tablet since God's name is not mentioned therein.

A very interesting comment is offered by our Sages regarding the time when the Israelites stood before Mount Sinai and said '*na'aseh venishma*' 'We will do and we will listen' (Exodus 24:7). God called the Angel of Death and said to him: 'Although I have given you power over all My creatures in the world, you can no longer do anything to My people Israel. The entire world is in your power, except for this nation'. To this the Angel of Death asked: 'Did you not create me for this purpose to take the life of all humans?' God responded: 'I created you to destroy other nations but not Israel for they are now accepting willingly my Torah.' The Sages based this idea on an allusion to the verse: 'and the writing was the writing of God, engraved upon the Tablets' (ibid. 32:16 – instead of reading '*charuth*' ('engraved') on the Tablets they read '*cheruth*' ('free') since because of the merit of the Torah, Israel became free of the Angel of Death (Midrash Rabbah). However, when they made the Golden Calf and were not worthy of receiving the Tablets written by God they lost this precious gift.

Following the breaking of the Tablets by Moses and before his prayers for forgiveness on behalf of the Israelites, God informs him that He wishes to destroy the nation and that from Moses He will make a great nation (Exodus 32:10). The Midrash offers us Moses' response. He said to God: 'If you destroy this nation which has the merit of the three patriarchs Abraham, Isaac and Jacob, I will be ashamed to stand before them; for they will say: "Look at what sort of a leader he was. He was concerned for his own good and not for that of Israel for he did not beseech mercy for them."' Moses then continued to plead for the people saying: 'Now, if you would, please forgive that sin. If not, blot me out from the Book that You have written' (ibid. 32). Moses argued as follows: 'If You do not forgive them their sin, let not my name be written in the Torah, for people will say I have spoken falsely. I taught them that if one repents You will accept it. Now if You do not forgive then they will argue that repentance is to no avail.'

The Siftei Cohen explains that the Book which Moses was referring to was not the Torah but the Book of the first man, Adam. This Book rewards every generation and its leaders until the time of Messiah. Moses' plea was to be erased from this Book 'in which You showed me to be a great leader. Since You wish to destroy them, what good is it that I am their leader? Moreover if you obliterate my generation, You must also obliterate the generation of Joshua and all the other generations that are destined to follow me in the world'.

Moses put in a further plea. He asked what the people had used to make the '*egel hazahav*'? Was it not with gold? 'To some degree it was Your fault because You gave them so much gold with which they made the idol.' Rabbi Hiyya ben Abba said: 'It is like the case of a man who had a son, he bathed him, anointed him and offered him plenty to eat and drink and hung a purse around his neck and set him down at the door of a brothel. How could the boy not sin?' (T. Berachot 32a).

Perhaps we can sum up the far-reaching importance of the Ten Commandments by quoting the late Chief Rabbi Dr. J. H. Hertz: 'The Revelation (at Mount Sinai) was the most remarkable event in the history of humanity; a sublime summary of human duties upon all mankind and cannot be antiquated as long as the world exists'.

Let us now turn to the custom of reading the Ten Commandments in the service on Shabbat morning. In many congregations when the Ten Commandments are read in the synagogue the congregation stands. It is interesting that there was a time when the '*Aseret Hadibrot*' was part of the daily morning service when the Temples existed. The Mishna Tamid 5:1 says that following the various morning duties performed by the priests in the Temple there was an order of the prayer service. I now quote: 'The superintendent would say to the Cohanim: "Recite the prayer beginning with Ahavah Rabbah before the Shema and then read the Ten Commandments followed by the three paragraphs of the Shema."' From this we learn that the Ten Commandments were an integral part of the Temple service and were said standing.

The Gemara in Berachot 12a confirms this custom and says that the people wished to follow the same tradition outside the Temple in the provinces but they were stopped from doing so on account of the arguments of the heretics who would attempt to convince the ordinary people that only the Ten Commandments were given by God to Israel. The communities of Sura and Nehardea sought also to do the same but were prevented from doing so for the same reason.

In the nineteenth century, an archaeologist by the name of Nash purchased some papyrus fragments known as the Nash papyrus which date back to the second century BCE. In it, mention is made of the Ten Commandments followed by the Shema, giving evidence to confirm that the '*Aseret Hadibrot*' were recited in Egyptian congregations at that time.

Whilst today the Ten Commandments are still not recited in our morning prayers, because of their importance, in many prayer books they are found at the end of the morning service and recited privately.

It was mentioned earlier that some people stand when the Ten Commandments are read publicly: this custom is not universal. It has been said that the late Chief Rabbi of Israel, the Rishon Lezion, Rabbi Ovadia Yosef, ruled against people standing up, in order not to give the impression that one section of the Torah is given greater honour than any other part of the Torah. So the question arises: Which is the correct procedure – to stand or not to stand? Is it possible that people stand as they did in Temple times? The answer is we do not know. However, nowadays, it all depends on the '*minhag hamakom*' ('the custom of the place'). Those congregations who stand do so because they hold that these commandments were given to the entire Jewish nation directly by God, while those who sit are of the view that the whole Torah was the word of God even though many of the laws were spoken through the prophet Moses. Indeed, let us conclude with the words of our Sages: '*Zu vezu divrei elokim chayim*' 'Both represent the words of the Living God'.

52

Prophets and Their Prophecies

THOUSANDS of years have passed since the last prophets delivered their timeless messages to the kings, leaders and members of the Jewish people. Their orations have not only been preserved in the Hebrew language in which they were delivered but have influenced every generation by their impelling moral force.

What, we may ask, is the reason why their voices and messages are still of relevance for us today and read almost weekly in the Haftarot on Shabbat and Yom Tov?

The answer is truly simple and short. Prophecy in Judaism was a divine inspiration, a manifestation of revelation granted by God to those whom He chose to proclaim His message of faith and trust in Him alone.

The institution of prophecy was based on this belief that God appoints individuals whom He considers fit to convey His will to others. As His appointed messengers, these individuals were called upon to receive and impart the Divine Will to all regardless of whether or not they wished to hear it.

The Rabbinic view of prophecy was based on two main principles. Firstly, that Moses was 'the father of all prophets' and that no other prophet either before or after him succeeded as he in penetrating God's glory and exploring the nature of God's attributes. The Torah, speaking in God's name, states: 'My servant Moses with him do I speak mouth to mouth, in a clear vision and not in riddles, at the image of the Lord does he gaze' (Numbers 12:6–8). This idea is further expressed in the Talmud by comparing the vision of the other prophets with that of Moses: 'All the prophets saw blurred images which does not shine as clearly as Moses who looked through a clear glass' (Yebamot 49b). In other words, the other prophets only imagined that they saw their visions clearly whilst Moses saw through a clear lens.

The second principle was that the prophets were not responsible for any new religious doctrines. Their function lay in bringing home the moral and ethical teachings of the Torah and the need to be loyal to the God of Israel alone.

The Sages explain the text: 'These are the commandments which the Lord commanded Moses for the children of Israel on Mount Sinai' (Leviticus 27:34) to mean that since the giving of the Torah, no prophet could make innovations to add to or take away from what is written therein (Shabbat 104a; Megillah 14a).

Though the prophets were called upon to be God's spokesmen, they were often reluctant to accept their calling. The first to do so was Moses who, when approached by God to go to redeem the Israelites from Egyptian bondage, replied: '*Mi anochi ki elech el Paro vechiotzi et bnei Yisrael mimitzrayim*'. 'Who am I that I should bring out the children of Israel from Egypt?' (Exodus 3:11).

The story of Jeremiah's call and his reluctance to accept it is quoted in the first chapter: 'The word of the Lord came unto me saying: "Before I formed you in the belly I knew you, and before you came forth out of the womb I sanctified you. I have appointed you a prophet unto the nations." Then said I: "O, Lord. Behold I know not how to speak, for I am a child"' (1:4ff).

The prophet Isaiah also expresses, when called upon, his unfitness to undertake his ministry. This is his initial response: 'Woe is me! For I am undone, for a man unclean of lips am I' (6:4). Again, one reads that the prophet Jonah, when called upon by God to go to Nineveh and prophesy against her, is unwilling to do so and flees to Tarshish.

But why were the prophets initially so opposed to accept their mission? Why in the face of numerous assurances did they hesitate to accept the role assigned to them? There are a number of answers for this. Both Moses and Jeremiah refused because of their lack of eloquence and experience. Another explanation offered in the Midrash goes as follows: 'Jeremiah said to God: 'I cannot prophesy concerning the Jewish people. For which prophet went out to them whom they did not wish to slay? You appointed Moses and Aaron and did they not seek to stone them? You appointed Elijah, the hairy one, and they mocked and taunted him. You appointed for them Elisha and they ridiculed him saying: 'Go up, you baldhead! Go up, you baldhead!' So how can I satisfy Israel?' (Yalkut Shimoni 262).

Similarly, Moses felt inadequate because he was not eloquent. He says to God: '*Lo eesh devarim anochi*' – 'O Lord, I am not a man of words' (Exodus 4:10), implying it was impossible for one unskilled in eloquence to succeed in the task and to be able to lead the people. Once he had finally accepted the call, one reads how Moses, constantly receiving complaints, on one occasion cries out to God: 'Why have you brought this trouble on your servant? You put all this burden of all the people on me? Did I conceive them? Did I give them birth? ... If I have found favour in Your eyes ... do not let me face my own ruin' (Numbers 11:11–15).

Similarly, Elijah, following the historic scene on Mount Carmel when he brings back the people to God and learns that Jezebel, the wife of Ahab, wishes to kill him, says to God: 'Take my life, I am no better than my ancestors!' (I Kings 19:4). Again, Jeremiah on learning that his messages go unheeded and is publicly mocked, cries out: 'Cursed be the day I was born! May the day my mother bore me not be blessed! Cursed be the man who brought my father the news ... saying: "A child is born to you – a son. Why did I ever come out of the womb to see trouble and sorrow and to end my days in shame?"' (20:14,15,18). It was then a matter of self-preservation that made many of the other prophets hesitant and afraid. As history records, the prophetic burden was not easy to bear, and the life stories of the prophets were of anguish, ridicule, rejection and even death, as recorded in the cases of Isaiah and Jeremiah.

The prophets, besides serving as the mouthpiece of God delivering their messages, were also often pleading on behalf of the wicked. The first to do so was Abraham who, in his sympathy for the wicked inhabitants of Sodom and Gemorrah, has a unique dialogue with God in the hope that the merits of the few righteous should prevail in avoiding their impending destruction. In a similar manner Moses, on numerous occasions, intercedes on behalf of Israel. On one occasion, following the event of the Golden Calf, he pleads on behalf of the nation, saying: 'O this people have sinned a great sin, and have made them a god of gold. Yet now, if You will forgive their sin (I am content to live) and if not, blot me, I pray You, out of Your book which You have written' (Exodus 32:31,32).

The prophet Samuel also, on learning that the nation wished to have a king like the other nations, 'called up to God' (1 Samuel 12:18) in prayer that they not be punished for seeking a king and not relying on God. Intercession was then an integral part of the prophet's role as friend and helper.

The story of the Shunamite who, in her hour of need, turns to the prophet Elisha for help is just one example of his service to assist others in time of need. In this story Elisha, on learning that she is childless, prays for her to have a son. One day when the child grew up and went to the field during the harvest, he died. On being informed of this Elisha goes to the parents' home and places himself upon the lad and finally brings him back to life (2 Kings 4:14–37). This and many other stories are related in the second book of Kings.

Let us consider now the role of the prophets and their prophecies. First among them was Amos. He saw for himself that outwardly people appeared religious. Sacrifices were offered freely, tithes were paid even more frequently than prescribed (4:4–5; 5:5). New moons and Shabbat were scrupulously kept (8:5) and the solemn assemblies observed. However, the ways in which the well-to-do were acquiring their wealth were highly anti-social. The poor man could not obtain justice at law and as a result were being pressed down economically. When it came to worship in the Temple, for all its enthusiasm it had no influence on behaviour as immorality was prevalent and forms of worship were open to the charge of idolatry. In the midst of this decadent civilisation, Amos turns upon the people: 'Thus says the Lord: "For three transgressions of Israel, yes for four, I will not turn away; because they sold the righteous for silver, and the needy for a pair of shoes ... they turn aside the way of the meek and a man and his father go to the same maiden to profane My holy name"' (2:6–8). In this passage Amos declares that God rejects the worship of Israel because it is not offered in the true spirit of religion.

Hosea is the first prophet to apply to Israel's relations with God in a metaphor of marriage. God had taken Israel to be His wife. Everything that a loving husband could do He had done for her but Israel did not reciprocate this love. He records a similar situation in his own domestic tragedy where he married a profligate woman who fled from his house and became a slave concubine of another. Because of his love for her, he buys her back from slavery and returns her home. He sees, as if in his own domestic tragedy and experience, a symbolic story of Israel's relation with God. God had redeemed Israel from Egyptian slavery, showered his love on them by making them and giving them the land of Israel. Yet with all this they repaid Him with ingratitude. In the end, Hosea offers the message of God's unwavering love to Israel and calls on them: 'Turn you to your God, keep mercy and justice and trust in God continually' (12:7).

In numerous passages of the prophetic books, we are told that God rejects the idea of sacrifices. But how could that be? One half of the book of Vayikra – Leviticus – deals with sacrifices and throughout the first and second Temples we know that the offering of sacrifices was an integral part of the priestly duties. The answer is explained by many prophets. Samuel, for example, on learning that King Saul had offered sacrifices following his smiting of the Amalekites, but failed to kill Agag, the king of the Amalekites, as he had been commanded to do, addresses Saul. 'Has the Lord as great delight in burnt offerings and sacrifices as in hearing the voice of the Lord? Behold, to obey is better than sacrifice, and to hear than in the fat of rams. For rebellion is as the sin of witchcraft, and stubbornness is as idolatry with its images' (1 Samuel 15:22,23). In these few words, Samuel summarises the true ethical teachings of the prophets. It expressed in the clearest terms the superiority of obedience over ritual worship. Offerings have only conditional value. They are brought to further the highest aim in life – the fulfilment of God's will. Something offered to the contrary is not brought in the right spirit of the Law and cannot be acceptable.

The prophets considered that the cornerstone of the community life was to be social righteousness. They therefore spoke out against social injustice and corruption. In their message they called for justice and human equality and defended the oppressed poor against the aristocracy and ruling class. The prophetic ideal of equality and outward insincere offerings of sacrifices were condemned. To quote Jeremiah: 'Will you steal, murder and commit adultery, and swear falsely, and offer unto

Baal ... and come and stand before Me in this house, whereupon My name is called and say: "We are saved!"' (7:10)

Let us conclude by stating that the prophets, by the loftiness of their character and the purity of their life, were not just messengers of doom. Through their timeless messages of hope and vision of restoration they offered the Jewish nation the prophetic promise of Israel's rebirth and future redemption. This is best illustrated in the vision of Ezekiel in the parable of the dry bones. This vision of the dry bones coming to life is directed to Israel's ultimate future: the miracle of Israel's national revival and the restoration that will take place. Quoting the prophet: 'Thus says the Lord God: "Behold, I will open your graves, and cause you to come up out of your graves, O My people; and I will bring you into the Land of Israel. And you shall know that I am the Lord, when I have opened your graves, and caused you to come up out of your graves, O My people. And I will put My spirit in you, and you shall live, and I will place you in your own land; and you shall know that I, the Lord, have spoken and performed it, says the Lord"' (Ezekiel 37:12–14).

53

The Book of Job

THE PROBLEM of reconciling human suffering with God's justice is an age-old one and the entire Book of Job is devoted to it.

We will attempt to survey how the book of Job was read and understood by our Sages in rabbinic literature. Ever since the book was written by Moses some 3500 years ago (Talmud Bavli, Baba Batra 15a) people have been attracted to the story of one who fell from a state of happiness to utmost misery and degradation. Indeed, the personality of Job exercised the minds of the Rabbis as is evidenced by the large number of *aggadot* (narratives/stories) about him and in the different opinions expressed in the Talmud.

One of the views expressed as to the reason for his suffering is that he was one of the three men whom Pharaoh consulted over how to deal with the problem of the multiplication of the Jewish people in Egypt. One counsellor, Balaam, advised the slaying of the male children. As a result, he himself was slain. Jethro, the future father-in-law of Moses, advised against harming them and as a result had to flee for his life. Job, the third counsellor, was silently undecided and for that he was sentenced to suffering (T.B. Sotah 11a).

The book can be divided into three sections: a beginning or prologue; Job and his three friends; the conclusion or epilogue.

Beginning

The book opens with the account of Job as a prosperous and pious man. He lived in the land of Uz which some scholars identify with Moab, which is Jordan today. He was blessed with seven sons and three daughters and his wealth consisted primarily of livestock and slaves. One day, unknown to Job, Satan the Accuser complained to God that the only reason why Job was so pious was because of his wealth and family, but if deprived of them he would surely denounce the Lord to His face. God agreed to Satan's request to test Job.

In a series of calamities, Job lost his cattle, possessions and all his ten children in one day. On hearing the dreadful news, he rent his garments, shaved his head, fell down on the ground and in his worship of God said: 'Naked I came out of my mother's womb, and naked shall I return there; the Lord gave and the Lord has taken away; blessed be the name of the Lord (ibid. 1:20–22).

The resourceful Satan now turned again to God and requested that if Job were offered a severer test he would surely turn away from serving Him. He said to God: 'Put forth your hand now and touch his bone and his flesh, surely he will blaspheme you to your face' (2:5) To which God replied: 'Satan, behold, he is in your hand; only spare his life '(ibid. v. 6). Satan then smote Job but still he did not sin with his lips (2:10). To his wife who said to him 'Blaspheme God and die', he replied: 'You speak as one of the impious women speaks. What? Shall we receive good at the hand of God and shall we receive not evil?' (ibid. 10).

Job and his friends

Shortly after this, under the impact of severe pain, Job turned from being a submissive saintly sufferer into a rebel. He cursed the day of his birth and longed for a way out of the terrors of life (ch. 3). In anguish he cried out: 'Why did I not die whilst in the womb? Why did I not perish at birth?' (ibid. 11).

Following his lament and the bitterness of his soul, the book deals with a series of three cycles of dialogues between Job and his three friends. These friends – Eliphaz, Bildad and Zophar – came from afar to comfort him in his misery, but they proved to be no comforters; for they proclaimed that God exercised His providence in this world. He rewarded the just and punished the wicked. They explained that Job's sorrowful fate was an indication of his guilt and advised him to accept God's divine justice and admit his wrongdoings.

But Job did not accept their advice and accusations, and protested his righteous name. He claimed that he was innocent and ready to face God. In protesting his integrity, he said to God; 'Do not condemn me. Tell me why you contend with me ... You know I am not guilty!' (ibid. 10:1,27) These were strong words indeed. But affirming once again his integrity, he pleaded elsewhere: 'Here is my signature, let the Almighty answer me!' (ibid. 31:35)

Not only did Job protest the punishment he did not deserve but he related how he concerned himself with the welfare of widows and orphans. He would visit the sick, both rich and poor, and when necessary he would bring a physician along with him. If the sick could not be healed, he would sustain the stricken family with advice and consolation. In this manner he would earn the blessing of the sick and the gratitude of the family (see 31:32). Furthermore, he would clothe the needy and open his house to the stranger and never rejoiced at the fall of those who hated him (ibid.). Yet Job's pleas were to no avail. His three friends were convinced that he had incurred divine punishment on account of his sins and were prepared to leave him to his fate.

Following this, a fourth young friend, Elihu, entered the debate. In four speeches he showed that suffering was the consequence of wrongdoing and rejected Job's rebellious assertion of God's injustice. He concluded his words by showing Job that God's works were wondrous and therefore 'men do fear Him' (ibid. 37:24).

After this, in a dramatic turn of events, the Almighty answered Job out of the whirlwind. In two speeches (38:1–40:2; 40:6–41:26), God revealed to Job the marvellous order of the universe, while completely bypassing Job's quest for an explanation of his sufferings.

Speaking of His creation, God declared that everything belonged to Him. yes, the earth, the sea, light and darkness, snow and hail, wind and rain, the lion and the raven, the ostrich, the hawk and the vulture, the ox and the wild ass, the hippopotamus and the crocodile. Everything was His, so who was he, Job, to demand an answer? What was his intention to contend with God? After hearing of God's response, Job's rebellion now subsided. He turned to God in humility saying 'I am of small account; what shall I answer You? I lay my hand upon my mouth' (ibid. 40:1,2).

God again, a second time, turned to Job, saying: 'Will you question My judgment? Will you condemn Me, so that you may justify yourself?' (ibid. 7). Job, finally full of remorse, turned to God and acknowledged: 'I know that You can do everything ... I have uttered that which I did not understand ... (Before) I had heard of You by the hearing of the ear; but now my eyes see You. Wherefore I abhor my words and report, seeing I am dust and ashes' (ibid. 42:2,5,6).

Conclusion

Following Job's repentance, God chastised his three friends for having misjudged Job and called upon them to go to him and seek his forgiveness, as well as to ask him to pray for them. Job did so and was now returned to good health.

Before long Job's fortunes were restored. He was once again blessed with seven sons and three daughters and with great wealth. He lived a long and full life and was blessed to see his sons and his sons' sons, even to the fourth generation.

Now let us consider Job's tribulations in the light of Talmudic-Midrashic tradition. The day of Job's accusation by Satan was Rosh Hashanah – the New Year's Day when God judges the good and the evil deeds of man (Targum on Job 1:6). Satan wished God to judge Job, not on his merits as this was, he claimed, to be due to the blessings conferred upon him. However, if personal suffering were imposed upon him, Satan argued, let us see Job's response as to whether he would still be pious in his ways. In imposing physical pain in which Job opens himself to outbursts and protests of his innocence, the atmosphere of divine justice prevails 'as long as Job stands against his friends and his friends against him'. The Gemara explains that while he may be excused for his rebellion since 'man is not held responsible for things done under duress' (T.B., Baba Batra 15a) yet there were signs of weakness and imperfection in his demands for redress. The turning point came when Job acknowledged his lack of understanding of God's goodness and His providence in the world. In making peace and praying for his friends, the Lord changed his fortunes and restored him to his previous state of well-being.

What is the meaning and message of the Book?

Here are some responses. To some Sages, Job is regarded as one of the truly God-fearing men of his time and the most pious gentile who ever lived (Midrash Deuteronomy Rabba 2:4). Though he served God out of love, which is the highest possible motivation (Gemara Sotah 30b), yet his questioning of God's justice, according to Maimonides, showed his defective understanding of God's ways. It was only after he attained a true philosophical knowledge of God from the whirlwind (Job 38–42) that he realised how presumptuous it was of man to question God's justice.

What did the author of Job mean to teach us? There are a wide variety of views on this. Here are the main ones:

1. That there does not necessarily have to be a connection between suffering and being a sinner. Suffering can often be merely a divine test of man's piety and not a punishment of sin.
2. The question of man's lot as contrasted with his rightful deserts is one which God alone decides, as He alone knows and records the thoughts and actions of man.
3. Suffering need not lead to isolation from God. Divine revelation is itself an act of grace and one must learn to endure his fate and trust in God's righteousness and to honour Him at all times.
4. Man cannot match God's power and wisdom for only then can he grasp the workings of God's providence. In other words, God cannot be judged because of our limited perspectives on life.
5. Finally, it is impossible to comprehend God's infinite benevolence and justice with our human finite minds. In the words of Pirkei Avot 'It is beyond our power to understand why the wicked are at ease or why the righteous suffer' (4:15). Indeed, the ways of God are a mystery and only through faith and humility can one hope to discern the meaning and beauty of life in all its forms.

54

Song of Songs

W HEN SOLOMON ascended the throne of his father, King
David, there was peace in the land. David wished to build a
Holy Temple to God and turned to the prophet Natan
saying: 'See now, I dwell in a house of cedar, but the Ark of God
dwells within the "curtain".' And Natan said to the King: 'Go do all that
is in your heart, for the Lord is with you' (2 Samuel 7: 2, 3).

That night, however, God appeared to Natan with the message that
David would not build the Temple. In the words of the Chronicle: 'You
have shed blood abundantly and you have made great wars. You shall
not build a House to My Name' (1:22:8). 'But, I will set up your seed
after you ... he will build a House for My Name' (2 Samuel 7: 12, 13).

On this response our Sages ask: 'But what of David's desire to erect
a temple to which the prophet Natan speaking in God's name told him
to do so? How does one resolve the contradiction of the two verses?'
The answer is that whilst David would not himself build it, the temple
built by Solomon would be called the House of David (Midrash
Shocher Tov). Since David had dedicated his entire life to the service of
God and accumulated material for its construction, the Temple would
be named after him. The Bible records that on the day when the Bet
HaMikdash was consecrated, the doors to its entrance would not open.
It was only when this verse was recited: 'Because for the sake of David'
that they opened. Thus, the Temple was called the House of David and
was dedicated by a special psalm known as the Psalm of David (30:1).

Solomon assumed the throne of his father when he was twelve years
old and in the fourth year of his reign commenced the construction of
the Temple which was to last four hundred and ten years. Solomon,
unlike his father, lived a life of luxury and pleasure. In Ecclesiastes we
are told: 'I did not deprive myself of all joy, for my heart was glad in all
my work and success' (2:10). Yet, Solomon was not like any other
king. He was one who could enjoy a life of physical pleasure and still

be aware of the true meaning of human existence. For him, physical indulgence and luxury did not turn him away from his love of God. This is best seen in the books ascribed to him in which he displays deep attachment to his Creator. From among the three holy works that he wrote, Proverbs, Song of Songs and Ecclesiastes, though each was holy, yet, say our Sages, 'Song of Songs is the Holy of Holies'.

This holy work and one which Rabbi Akiva called 'holy of holies' could only be produced by one who has risen above the enjoyments of the physical world and seeks to cleave to his Maker. This song, which is an allegory of the deep love which God has for His people and which was completed on the day of the Temple's dedication, inspired Rabbi Akiva to exclaim: 'The world was not worthy of the day when "Song of Songs" was composed.' The Zohar further states in the name of Rabbi Yosi: 'There was no greater joy before the Holy One, blessed be He, from the day the world was created than on that day'.

So what is the essence of this song? Unlike those who see it as a physical relationship between a man and woman, our Rabbis understand it as a close attachment that exists between Israel and God. God and Israel are bound together, one to another, and this song is a manifestation of the great love and joy which God has for us, His people. This is indeed the highest form of love one can ever obtain.

Maimonides explains this idea in some detail. 'What is the path that leads to the love and fear of God? When one meditates upon God's wondrous and great deeds, and acknowledges His infinite wisdom, immediately he loves, praises, exalts and feels a great urge to attach himself to Him. As David said: "My soul thirsts after the living God"' (Yesodei Hatorah 2:2).

This is the purpose of man's role and mission – to recognise and use every physical aspect of his creation to attach himself to God. That is the deeper meaning of love in an allegorical sense as expressed by Solomon in Song of Songs. If we as human beings could understand the greatness of our Creator and benefactor, our love for Him would be one of intimate spiritual attachment. This is what our teachers called 'Cleaving to God'.

In composing this song, Solomon foresaw that the Jewish people were destined to suffer in numerous exiles and would feel abandoned by

God's love. This is the meaning of the verse; 'May He kiss me with the kiss of His mouth' (1:2) which Rashi explains: 'The exiled Israel turns to God in her widowhood and pleads that He be intimate with her again and continue to communicate the innermost secrets of the Torah.' Having been separated he calls out 'Sustain me in exile ... for I am sick with love' (ibid.). Israel in Galut says to the Holy One, blessed be He: 'All the sufferings that you bring upon me are for the purpose of making me more beloved by you.' In this passionate plea, Israel reminds God to continue to love us in exile and dwell in our midst until we are finally reunited.

The Jewish nation is constantly aware of the sin of the Golden Calf. This unfaithfulness on their part kindled God's anger to destroy them, but because of His love, as a husband to his wife, He forgave them. This is the meaning of the verse: 'Behold You are beautiful, my beloved indeed pleasant' (1:16). Israel responds to God: 'The greatness is not ours but Yours for having pardoned that sin and let the Divine Presence continue to dwell amongst us' (Rashi).

At the end of the book, the Almighty responds: 'Flee, my beloved, from the exile, you who dwells in far flung gardens ... Let me hear that you will sanctify Me' (8:14). Dispersed in the diaspora tending the gardens of others God awaits the day when Israel will return once again to Jerusalem, the holy city where the third Temple will be rebuilt.

Throughout this holy work, King Solomon writes the relationship between God and Israel to that of a loving and devoted husband to a wife who has strayed. In this dialogue, Israel admits its faults and seeks to endure herself to Him. The Holy one in them proclaims His unwavering attachment to the congregation of Israel and awaits her return to Him. It is with this hope of final redemption that Solomon concludes his song.

55

Pharisees and Sadducees

URING the period of the Second Temple, a number of
religious and political parties existed in Israel. The critical
times through which the Jews had passed following the
Maccabean revolt and the stand taken by the people against the
influence of Hellenism played a major role in the emergence of two
distinct groups known as the Pharisees and Sadducees.

The word '*Pharisee*' is derived from the Hebrew '*parash*' to be
separated or 'separated ones'. In the *Arukh*, the only medieval lexicon
covering the Talmudic- midrashic literature by Rabbi Nathan ben
Yehiel, the name means 'one who separates himself from all
uncleanness'. Thus '*Pharisee*' would mean 'those who separated
themselves by avoiding contact with others for reasons of ritual purity'
(see *Kiddushin* 66a). As a religious party during the Second Temple
they emerged as a distinct group shortly after the Hasmonean revolt,
around 165 BCE.

The *Pharisees* were the successors of the *Hasidim*, an earlier Jewish
group who were meticulous in the observance of Jewish ritual and the
study of the Torah. As the traditional followers of the Prophets, they
upheld the validity of the '*Torah Shebaal Peh*' as well as the '*Torah
Shebichtav*'.

By the first century CE they imbued the majority of the nation with
the spirit of holiness and observance of the Torah through study and
prayer. So important did they value religious observance that they were
willing to accept foreign domination as long as it did not interfere with
their inner way of life.

It was due to the progressive tendencies of their interpretation of the
Bible, which they based on the Prophets and handed down by tradition,
that they developed a system of hermeneutics which would make
Judaism a living force. To give one example, the Biblical command
states: 'If one harms another, then you shall give life for life, eye for

eye, tooth for tooth, hand for hand' (Exodus 21:23–24) This was not to be taken literally as retaliation or measure for measure but as monetary compensation to the injured party.

The Pharisees believed and taught that God was involved in Divine retribution and that man was granted free will to choose between good and evil. They further believed in the resurrection of the dead and the immortality of the soul.

Unlike the *Sadducees* who believed that God took no active role in human affairs, the Pharisees held that God's Providence was manifest in ordinary daily events and that man had it in his power to choose between good and evil. Their doctrine was that God's foreknowledge of ethical conduct does not predetermine man's actions, good or bad, as 'everything is foreseen, yet freedom of choice is given' (*Avoth* 3:1b). This belief in man's responsibility for his actions led to the *Pharisaic* doctrine of divine retribution.

The Pharisees further believed in the resurrection of the dead and based this doctrine on Biblical utterances of the prophets: 'Your dead shall live, their corpses shall arise' (Isaiah 26:19). 'I will open your graves and bring you out of your graves' (Ezekiel 37:12).

The Pharisees further held that the soul and the body would in the future world be reunited and would stand in judgment before God and receive reward or punishment according to their conduct during their lifetime.

According to the Talmud, the word '*Sadducees*' is derived from Zadok, a high priest in the days of Solomon who was entrusted with the control of the Temple. Descendants of this family constituted the Temple hierarchy down to the Second Temple, who opposed the Pharisees down to the destruction of Jerusalem in 70 CE.

The Sadducean group was a party composed largely of priests and aristocrats. They believed that Temple worship and its rites were paramount in service to God and they held in highest regard the sacrificial cult. They opposed the Pharisees' belief in the 'Oral Law', denied the resurrection, immortality of the soul and the advent of a Messiah.

The Pharisees, in holding that both the Written and the Oral Law were given to Moses, therefore placed great importance upon Torah study and synagogue worship. They taught that since God was to be found everywhere, He could be worshipped both inside and outside the Temple and was not to be addressed by sacrifices alone. They thus promoted the Synagogue as a place of worship, study and prayer and made it a central and important place in the life of the nation.

Since the Sadducees had made Temple worship central to Jewish life, after its destruction in 70 CE this group ceased to exist. On the other hand, with the fall of the Temple, the Pharisaic emphasis on education and the important role of the Synagogue led to the continuation of religious survival to this very day.

56

Babylonian Jewry

THE JEWISH community of Babylon (Iraq) can be dated back to the exile of Judeans from Palestine by the Babylonian King Nebuchadnezzar in 597 BCE. Following the destruction of the First Temple and the loss of statehood, many of the leading nobles, together with others, were deported to Babylon where they settled along the 'Two Rivers', the Tigris and the Euphrates. Their initial reaction to living in a foreign land is expressed by the Psalmist: 'By the rivers of Babylon there we sat and wept when we remembered Zion...If I forget you, O Jerusalem, let my right hand forget her cunning.' (137:1,5)

The history of this community, which became one of the largest, most prominent and most influential in shaping Jewish life, has been well documented. From the beginning of the sixth century BCE until the thirteenth century CE, Babylonia became the centre of Jewish life. Next to the Jewish centres of learning in Palestine, Babylon produced a strong infrastructure of Jewish life. The crown jewels were the three important Yeshivot of Sura, Nehardea and Pumbeditha. At the head of these academies were great scholars who guided the people in the study and observance of Jewish Law.

The study of the Torah was actively pursued both in Palestine and Babylon and from this there developed two distinct Talmuds. One is referred to as the Jerusalem Talmud, the other as the Babylonian Talmud. The project of compiling the latter was commenced in the beginning of the first half of the third century CE to the end of the fifth century. The former, though begun at around the same time, was finalised a century before. Though both Talmuds were studied diligently, the Babylonian Talmud in time gained supremacy and authority within the entire Jewish world.

Very few countries have experienced as many radical changes of empires and rulers as Babylon. This land saw the rise and fall, growth and decline of dynasties and nations. Until the rise of the Islamic

175

Caliphate from 634 to 1258, the Jews of Babylon enjoyed relative peace and tranquillity, allowing the community to thrive and prosper as well as to serve as the world centre of Torah. In addition, they were granted a good deal of political autonomy and were proud of having in their midst a Jewish Exilarch known as the '*Resh Galuta*' who could trace his ancestry back to the Royal Dynasty of King David. As the head of the community recognised by the government, he was authorised to collect the taxes of the Jewish people and to transfer all monies to the authorities. As a dispenser of justice, he was further empowered to appoint judges and to impose fines, flogging and imprisonment.

The heads of Babylonian academics were selected for their office by prominent scholars but had to be ratified by the exilarch. They were referred to as 'Heads of yeshivah' 'Rashei Yeshivah'.

Due to the incalculable influence these Rabbinical Academics had on the teachers and students, the prayer 'Yekum Purkan' is still recited as part of the Sabbath morning services. Composed in Arameic it reads: 'May salvation from heaven... be granted unto the teachers and rabbis of the holy community, who are in the land of Israel and in the land of Babylon and in the lands of our dispersion etc. ... may the King of the universe bless them, prolong their lives and may they be saved and delivered from every trouble and mishap'.

The glory of Babylonian Jewry began to decline with the Mongol invasion in the thirteenth century and with Islamic discrimination against Jews in the Middle Ages. This caused the large Babylonian Yeshivot to dwindle and led to the migration of Torah scholars to other lands. One cannot conclude a historical sketch of this once vibrant community without at least mentioning two amongst the many distinguished *Geonim* (Heads of the Academies) of the tenth and eleventh centuries and fast forwarding to an outstanding luminary Sage of the nineteenth century.

A renowned scholar of the tenth century was Rabbi Hai Gaon, whose name is closely connected with the liturgical practice of Babylonian Jewry which differs greatly from all other rites. Among his many 'Responsa' are matters dealing at length with the customs and usages of the community. The other outstanding Sage was Rabbi Sherira Gaon, who traced his pedigree to the family of the Exilarchs.

Among his writings is his famous '*Iggeroth*' letters which deal with an accurate account of the development of the Oral Law, and a detailed chronology of the Tannaim, Amoraim, Saburaim and Geonim.

In the nineteenth century a new star arose who, from his early days, was destined for greatness. His name was Yosef Haim, later to be known by the famous title '*Ben Ish Hai*'. His grandfather was Rabbi Moshe Haim who served as the Rabbi of Baghdad for fifty years.

Haham Yosef Haim, from a young age, was recognised by the Rabbis as a holy man and Torah giant. Born in 1859, he was elected at the young age of twenty-six as spiritual leader of the Jews in Iraq. During his lifetime, he was recognised throughout the Far East for his scholarship. The fruits of his scholarship can be seen from the forty or so scholarly works that have been printed. These works show, on the one hand, his industry and learning, and on the other hand his great influence on the religious life and practice of Babylonian Jewry. Until this day, he is revered as one of the greatest Torah Sages who have lived during the last two centuries.

Returning to our subject, one finds that from the sixteenth century, when the region came under the rule of the Ottoman Empire, until around 1932 when Iraq became an independent state, there was relative peace for the Jews. However, with the establishment of Medinat Yisrael in 1948, Jews there were subjected to discrimination – persecution, confiscation of their worldly possessions and even death.

As a result, from the 1950's, this community after two and a half millennia were forced to leave empty-handed. From an approximate population of one hundred and twenty thousand in 1948, there are left today just a handful of Jews. Fortunately, they have moved to parts of the Western world with the majority living in Israel where they are fully integrated into the general stream of society.

57

A Short History of the Marranos

THIS IS a short account of the origins and fate of those Spanish Jews who were known as the Marranos or Secret Jews of the Peninsula. It is a record of a period when they achieved prominence socially, politically and economically, but were suspected of a secret adherence to Judaism.

Crypto-Judaism, in one form or another, dates back to the very beginning of Judaism. The official attitude as taught by the Sages of the Talmud was clear. One may and should save one's life if the occasion demanded, excluding however the three cardinal sins of idolatry, murder and incest. If one was called upon to commit any one of these three offences, then death should be preferred.

Jewish law thus made provision for cases when observance of ceremonial practices could not be observed, such as in times of persecution, referred to as '*Shaat HaShemad*'. In such times Judaism was driven underground and practised in secret. If and when, the opportunity arose for Jews to be able to revert to their ancestral faith, these apostate Jews, known as '*Anusim*', were treated by the Rabbis in a lenient manner.

The term '*Anusim*' was applied not only to the forced converts themselves but also to their descendents who clandestinely cherished their Jewish faith by attempting to observe at least some vestiges of customs and mitzvot. These original converts known as '*Conversos*' or 'New Christians', though accepted by the Church, were not favourably accepted by the urban society. By the end of the fifteenth century, outbreaks of popular animosity by Christian Ecclesiastics led to the Inquisition and the final expulsion of Jews from Spain in 1492. According to historical records, the original converts in Castille and Toledo alone numbered some thirty-five thousand Jews. They were followed by many other communities from around Spain.

Whilst a great number of the first generation of converted Jews became Christians, a vast majority of others remained completely Jewish even though outwardly they lived as Christians. They took their children to Church to be baptised but in their private homes were deeply attached to Judaism. They kept the Sabbath as far as it was in their power to do so, observed the dietary laws and, where possible, circumcised their baby boys. Thus, in race, belief and practice they remained as before their conversion.

Because they had outwardly embraced their new faith, they were able to integrate with all sections of society. The Law, Army, Universities, Finance and even the Church itself were over-run by these converts. In 1480, for example, the Supreme Court of Justice in Aragon was presided over by persons of Jewish extraction. It was said that within a couple of generations there was barely a single aristocratic family in Aragon, from the Royal House downwards, which was 'free from the taint of Jewish blood'. So in time the original Jewish converts with their descendents became considerable in number and by the fifteenth century were a serious threat to the Church.

Whilst the official policy of Roman Catholicism was against forced conversion, those original conversions were considered as valid. On the other hand, the Church authorities in the fifteenth century, realising that many of these adherents were not sincere, took measures to check the blasphemous duplicity of those who were only Christian in name. To add to this, feeling against them by the general population grew and led to these converts being called '*Marranos*' which in Spanish meant 'Swine'.

Moreover, the nobility detested these 'New Christians' partly for the above reasons, but also for their enterprise. For these New Christians were not just influential in the government, whilst holding high office at Court, but many of them were extremely wealthy.

The bitterness and tension led to street fights, attacks, burning of homes and in some cases to massacre. The Church, in the hope of restoring order, turned to inflicting punishment for heresy, a practice that was as old as the Church itself. Already in the days of the Roman Emperors Theodorius and Justinian, special tribunals were established for this purpose. In the hope of solving this problem the Church turned its attention to those it believed had relapsed into Judaism. Power was then handed over to the bishops who, by virtue of their office, were to hunt down and punish those guilty of heresy.

One of Queen Isabella of Spain's confessors at court was Thomas de Torquemada. He was totally opposed to the Marranos in spite of the fact that he himself was of Jewish extraction. Due to his influence on the Queen, and with the support of the ruling Pope Sixtus IV, full inquisitional powers were handed over to the Church authorities and to the Commissioners of the Dominican Order to commence their activities forthwith.

On 9 October 1480, a Royal Order was published which finally led to the establishment of the Inquisition. The procedure of the Inquisition was in theory based on a fair trial, but in fact everything connected to it took place under conditions of the greatest secrecy. All parties concerned, be they witnesses, accusers or accused, were sworn to the most profound confidence. The accusers and accused were never confronted and names of the accusers were suppressed. Thus, any attempt on the part of the prisoner to invalidate the evidence whilst his life was at stake had to be based upon utter conjecture. The system thus naturally lent itself to false accusations.

The most terrible weapon of the Inquisition, other than the power of inflicting the death penalty, was the right it enjoyed of confiscating the property of those it convicted. The victims of the Inquisition came from all sections of society, whether nobles, statesmen, merchants, craftsmen, farmers or workers. By confiscating their property and wealth, the Inquisitors had a weapon which struck at a man's entire family reducing him from affluence to poverty.

Added to this were other penalties. Anyone convicted by the Inquisition had their children and descendents excluded from holding any public office. They were not permitted to become doctors, lawyers, chemists or tutors of the young. They were further not permitted to dress in garments of gold or silver or to wear jewellery.

Space does not permit us to go into the Heroes and Martyrs who died at the stake and who, until the very end, performed '*Kiddush Hashem*' by reciting aloud the Shema. But a few words need to be said about the religion of the Marranos.

According to historians, the first generation of Marranos were knowledgeable in the Hebrew language, possessed Hebrew books and observed the dietary laws. They observed the Sabbath and Festivals and held private services in houses. When burials occurred, they would do their utmost to be buried near their unconverted fathers and observe the rites of mourning. The second and following generations however had no knowledge of Hebrew and based their religion on oral tradition handed down to them and the Latin version of the Bible.

Their observance of Jewish laws was minimal, but they held firmly to the Five Books of Moses as the true Law and the hope of the Messianic Return to the Land of Promise. The Book of Psalms in the Latin Vulgate Version of the Bible was accessible to them and became a perpetual store of spiritual comfort. They faced towards the East when praying and covered their heads with a white cloth instead of a Tallit. They firmly upheld the belief in the One God and the Brotherhood of Israel, hoping for the final deliverance of Israel.

Returning to the Inquisition and extent of the devastation achieved, thousands upon thousands of these '*Conversos*', the 'New Christians', were tortured and died at the stake. With the growing degradation and impoverishment of the Jews in general, on 30 March 1492 the decree for the expulsion of Jews from the whole of Spain was declared. Four months later, on 31 July, the history of the Marranos came to an end in Spain.

The historian Burke tells us: 'Two hundred thousand Spaniards, men, women and children, rich and poor, men of refinement and position, the aged, the sick and the infirm, all were driven and stripped of everything ... and thus North, South, East and West they went to find an uncertain abiding place.'

Fortunately, Divine Providence granted that these exiles found homes in other soils which took plant and flourished with time. Constantinople, Italy, Holland and England welcomed these refugees where today many of their descendents live.

The expulsion from Spain was motivated by bigotry and greed. Yet history shows that neither motive achieved its end. As shown by L. I. Newman in his book: *Jewish Influence on Christian Reform Movements*, forced conversions added to an element of Christian society and hastened the schism in the Church itself, which was to split in what became known as the Reformation. Neither did greed gain any enduring profit, for scarcely a hundred years elapsed from the expulsion before Spain suffered poverty directly for expelling the Jews.

In looking back on the calamities that befell the Jews of Spain, one ingredient becomes apparent: the steady, tenacious and indomitable courage that the Marranos held. In the face of torture and threat of death by burning they remained steadfast to their ancestral faith.

Christopher Columbus in his account of the expedition which led to the discovery of the New World wrote, 'In the same month in which their Majesties issued the edict that all Jews be driven out of their Kingdom and from its territories, in the same month they gave me order to undertake with sufficient men my expedition of discovery.' Setting sail as he did, within a day or two of the departure of the last Jewish exiles, many Marranos went with him on this expedition. Indeed, there are grounds to believe that Columbus himself was a member of the New Christian family and so a member of the race.

The Marranos were quick to realise the possibilities of the New World and in view of the difficulty of finding refuge in parts of Europe, turned naturally to America. Thus, not long after their arrival in New York, the Sephardi Synagogue 'Sheerith Yisrael' was built. Its very name 'The Remnant of Israel' was to be a reminder of those who survived the Holocaust in Spain.

Following their arrival in New York, other Marrano settlements were to be found in Southern America and Newport, Rhode Island. Thus, of the half-dozen Jewish congregations established in the United States before the War of Independence, practically all had been founded by Marranos themselves or by their descendents.

Thus, the circle of Marrano communities ranged from the countries of Africa to the Republic of the West. In their own history, they exemplify the saying: 'Against truth, Force does not avail.' The very fact that the Jews of Spain survived and finally prospered in other countries is indeed a living witness to the vitality of Judaism and human courage.

58

A History of Jewish Liturgy

THE PRACTICE of prayer is a very ancient institution which goes back to the very beginning of mankind. Before the people of Israel existed and prior to the age of the patriarchs Abraham, Isaac and Jacob, people engaged in prayer. The reason for this is that as Man became aware of the existence of an omnipotent and beneficent Creator and his own frailty, he addressed his supplications and praise to God.

When one turns to the Bible, there are many beautiful and sublime prayers recited by Moses, King David, King Solomon and the Prophets. However, the formula of regular Tefillah goes back to the Babylonian captivity, following the destruction of the First Temple. It was Ezra and the Men of the Great Assembly, known as the *Anshei Knesset Hagedolah* who, together with the most learned scholars of that age (such as the Prophets Haggai, Zechariah, Malachi and Daniel) instituted the morning, afternoon and evening services in lieu of the daily sacrifices when the Temple existed. They also arranged the '*Musafim*' prayers for the Sabbath and solemn days of the year. All these prayers were recited in the Classical Hebrew language apart from the Kaddish which was said in Aramaic, the language spoken at that time in Babylon. Further supplications were added for joyous or fast days or in times of suffering or danger.

Following the destruction of the Second Temple by the Romans in 70 CE, during the Talmudic Age (between 200 and 500 CE) several prayers were also added by the great Babylonian Sage Rav and later Geonim who were the Heads of the foremost Babylonian Academies from the seventh to the eleventh centuries CE. The first collection of the Prayer Book was the Siddur of Amram Gaon (ninth century) and it became the basis of our present-day liturgy.

The renowned ninth-century scholar Rav Saadia Gaon in his introduction to his prayer book writes: 'I have decided to assemble in this book the authoritative prayers, hymns and benedictions, in their original form as they existed before and after the exile... I shall also mention what I have learnt about additions or omissions according to the arbitrary opinions of individual groups... I have pointed out that they were unsupported by tradition.' By his work, he attempted to use his prayer book as a means to unify all Jews to a common denominator

Already during the Geonic period these developed into two distinct traditions known as the Palestinian and Babylonian Rites. The Palestinian Rite in time spread over Northern Europe and became known as the Ashkenazi Rite, whilst the Babylonian Rite spread to Spain, North Africa and the Near East. Basically, both traditions represented the standard prayers recited daily and varied mainly in the general wording of Kaddish, Kedushah and different versions of the Amidah in its nineteen blessings.

The main differences, when we turn to the Machzor for Rosh Hashanah or Yom Kippur, lie in the *piyyutim* (poetry) added to the prayers in a desire to give emphasis to the intense emotions and aspirations of the Jewish people. They were composed by the *paytanim* (poets) who drew their material from the inexhaustible wealth of ideas dispersed in the Psalms, Talmud and Midrash.

The earliest *paytanim* lived in Eretz Yisrael around the sixth century CE. By the commencement of the eleventh century, *piyyut* literature was to be found in places as far away as North Africa and the Iberian Peninsula. In Europe, *piyyut* literature appeared first in Southern Italy in the second half of the ninth century. By the tenth to the eleventh centuries, famous *paytanim* were to be found in Germany with Ashkenazi *piyyut* being produced by important composers such as Eliezer ben Kalir, Moses ben Kalonymus and Simon ben Isaac. Oriental *piyyut* began in the tenth century and some of the outstanding composers were Solomon Ibn Gabirol, Moses Ibn Ezra and Yehudah Halevi.

In the following centuries, various communities established their own distinctive collection of *piyyutim*. Among the Sephardi Iraqi communities for example, a special book called *Sefer Pizmonim*, a collection of praises and poetry, covers all aspects of daily, Sabbath, Holy Days and religious ceremonies. Similar works are to be found among the Ashkenazi Rite which have found their way into the prayer book and *machzor*.

In this brief study of Jewish liturgy, one learns that the Siddur and Machzor were not the product of an individual, a body or an age, but the growth of many centuries. It reflects the Jewish spirit and gives expression to the service of the heart through which we Jews communicate with our Father in Heaven.

59

Reflections on Jewish History

I WOULD like to share with you a bird's eye view of Jewish history. Following the destruction of the First Temple in 586 BCE and the Second Temple in 70 CE, the Jewish nation has been subjected to an alternating chain of periods of suffering and freedom.

Already in Sefer Devarim (4:20) the Torah warns Israel of direct punishment if we fail to live up to the ideals of being an '*Am Kadosh*', a Holy People. Moses tells us 'And the Lord shall scatter you among the nations.' On the other hand, the Almighty promised us everlasting existence by performing miracles for our people in times of danger and national disaster. The Prophet Isaiah (51:11), speaking to those going into exile after the fall of the first Temple, says: 'And the ransomed of the Lord shall return and come forth singing unto Zion. Everlasting Joy shall be upon their heads. They shall obtain gladness and joy. Sorrow and suffering shall flee away.' Indeed, with all the calamities that may befall us, redemption is sure to come. Commenting on the text: 'If fire breaks out ... he that kindles the fire shall surely make restitution' (Exodus 22:5) the Gemara explains this to mean that just as God kindles a fire, He will also build Jerusalem again 'with a wall of splendour' (Bava Batra 60b).

Shortly after the destruction of the first Jewish commonwealth when the Jews lived in Babylon, an event occurred which led to the fall of the Babylonian empire. The Persian King Cyrus changed the fortunes of the Jewish people. In the year 539 BCE, he issued an edict permitting Jews to return to their native land and rebuild the Temple in Jerusalem. Whilst the work was interrupted in between, through opposition from the Samaritans, it was completed by 516 BCE.

Due to the untiring efforts of Ezra the Scribe and Nehemiah, a strenuous reform and religious revival took place. For the next two centuries, a gradual evolution went on whereby the Sages under the Men of the Great Assembly, known as the '*Anshei Knesset*

HaGedolah', asserted themselves by establishing the Torah and its traditional teachings to the Jewish people.

Unfortunately, with the destruction of the Second Temple by the Romans and the total subjection of the nation, first by Titus and then – sixty years later in 135 CE – after the Bar Kochba revolt, the city of Jerusalem was ploughed up and renamed *Aelia Capitolina.*

The subsequent dispersion of the Jews throughout the Roman Empire brought with it not just interaction with paganism and barbarity on a large scale, but the general attitude of the gentiles towards the Jews as non-conformists. Our special covenant with God as His chosen people, the rite of circumcision, the observance of the Sabbath as a day of rest, the dietary laws and the forbidding of marriages with non-Jews, singled them out as being different from the others.

The question of anti-Semitism is still the subject widely debated in the early centuries following the dispersion of the Jews throughout the Roman Empire. Scattered abroad amongst the people of diverse backgrounds and though subjected periodically to jealousy and hatred, it seems that Jews did settle down and gained their living as weavers, goldsmiths and workers in iron and bronze. There were still others who were engaged in commerce and as merchants.

Fortunately, the Jewish community in Babylon under Persian rule flourished both materially and spiritually. Under the authority of the *Resh Galutah,* who was descended from the House of David, Jewish life flourished. By the end of the fifth century, under the influence of the great academies in Nehardea, Sura and Pumpedita, the Babylonian Talmud was published and reflected the intellectual treasures of learning which were to be preserved for posterity.

One finds that by the beginning of the third century, with the rise of Christianity, the idea of divine punishment against Jews was being expressed by some Church fathers. The theologian Origen, speaking of the role of Jews in the death of Jesus, writes: 'The Jews will not return to their earlier situation of being the chosen people, for they have committed the most abominable of crimes against the saviour of the human race.' Hence the city where Jesus suffered was necessarily destroyed, the Jewish nation was driven from its country and another people was called by God.

There was a noticeable rise of theological hatred against the Jews by the fourth century, particularly in the East. With the establishment of the Christian faith as the formal religion by Emperor Constantine in 313, a Byzantine tradition of anti-Semitism was established. There are numerous references to the fact that many Church councils expressed concern about the influence they were having on Christianity and the brethren were forbidden to eat or mingle with Jews.

However, from the eighth to the tenth centuries, with the rise of letter-writing, one learns of prosperous Jews who, because of their ability to speak Persian, Arabic, Greek, German and Spanish, engaged in all aspects of life and thought. From this it would appear that formal anti-Semitism, while promoted by bishops and other spiritual leaders, was not universally accepted by the common people. During this period, Jewish communities were granted broad religious autonomy. Talmud and general scholarship flourished in France and Germany and Jews founded guilds and international connections with fellow Jews in Europe.

Things began to change by the end of the eleventh century. On 27 November 1095, the Council of Clermont Ferrand under Pope Urban II began to preach the first Crusade which began a chain of events that had a catastrophic effect on Jews. Knights, monks and commoners left their homes, families and livelihood on a pilgrimage to conquer the Holy Land from the Muslims and the Jews. A spirit of pillage, massacre and persecution took its toll. Faced with the choice of conversion or death, many Jews resorted to suicide, with the Shema Yisrael on their lips.

Each time a Crusade was announced, swept by a movement of faith, each time Christians set out on a mission of conquest, the worse would be the fate of the Jews. Thus in 1183 with the Third Crusade, the sad events facing Jews in Europe reached the shores of England. Great massacres occurred in London, York, Norwich, Stamford and Lynn, fanned by the nobles and lords. The general pattern was always the same: looting, massacre and confiscation of property. One chronicler, Fruitoff, informs us, 'In the villages they traversed, the crusaders killed or baptised what remained of those impious Jews who are truly enemies of the church.'

Following the Golden Era of Spain which lasted for approximately two hundred years from the thirteenth to the fifteenth century when Jewish life prospered, Sephardi Jews enjoyed a happy relationship with the Arabs and Christians. This resulted in a growth of Jewish astronomers, medical men, philosophers and mathematicians who contributed not just to the Sephardi heritage of learning, but to the nation as a whole. Maimonides, Yehudah HaLevi, Yehudah ben Samuel and others composed many works on Judaism. Maimonides' fourteen volumes of Yad Hachazakah, a codification of Jewish law, is a legacy still studied by Rabbis and students alike.

This period of tranquillity and prosperity, however, was to change with the Black Death in 1347, known as the Black Plague. So catastrophic was this plague that in the space of three years, from 1347 to 1350, a third or more of the population of Europe was annihilated. This tragic event caused the destruction of much of Europe's Jewish community. What was the reason for this? A belief was spread that the plague was a Divine punishment to chastise Christians. Pollution of water, they believed, was brought about by the dregs of humanity such as the lepers and the Jews. As a result, Jews were made a scapegoat and many were killed in the Rhineland and in other neighbouring regions.

In Spain where a large number of Marranos lived, King Ferdinand and Queen Isabella, under the influence of the Church, embarked on the Inquisition which ended with the expulsion of all Jews in 1492. The historian U. R. Burke, in his *History of Spain*, informs us, '200,000 Spanish Jews, men, women and children, rich and poor, were all included in one common destruction and were driven, stripped of everything, from their peaceful homes, to die on their way to some less savage country. And so North, South, East and West, Jews struggled over Spain to find an uncertain abiding-place in neighbouring Africa.'

Between the fifteenth and nineteenth centuries, the history of the Jews in the Middle East and in Europe is well-documented. Suffice it to say that Jews in these countries were subjected to periods of favourable existence but also faced pogroms. So long as Christianity held unchallenged sway in Europe, Jews existed on the margin of European life.

But with the coming of the eighteenth-century 'Enlighten-ment', the status of the Jews was raised as a matter of debate. Many philosophers and humanists, in discussing the comparative virtues of the various religions, felt that all were equally good. There were others like Voltaire and his followers who pressed their view that Jews were ignorant by nature and could never be integrated into a modern society.

Nonetheless, through the *Haskalah* movement (a Hebrew term for Enlightenment) Jews in Europe regarded secular culture and philosophy as of central value which could assist in elevating the human and social value of the Jews. Unfortunately, this led to assimilation and many wealthy Jews taught their children secular studies instead of the Bible and Talmud.

It should be mentioned that the influence of Haskalah also penetrated into Orthodox circles. Some important and learned Rabbis, like Rabbi Ezekiel Landau, agreed that it was necessary to know language and writing, 'although Torah was to be the main thing'. The first integral school in which Jewish and general subjects were taught was opened in 1790 in Germany and it brought about a change in children's education.

In 1894, Alfred Dreyfus, an officer in the French army, was charged with treason. His court martial, conviction and ultimate acquittal had great repercussions in France and in the Jewish world. The Dreyfus case led Theodore Herzl, the father of political Zionism, who attended the trial as a news correspondent, to become convinced that the only solution to anti-Semitism was for the Jews to return to the land of Israel.

He had two aims in convening the First Zionist Congress in Basle in August 1897. Firstly, he wanted to establish the World Zionist Organisation as a political organisation of the Jewish people. Secondly, he wanted to see the establishment of a national home for the Jews in Eretz Yisrael. Until his death he worked tirelessly to achieve this. The motto of a book he wrote stated: 'If you will it, it is no dream.' This became the watchword of the entire Zionist movement.

Prophetically, Herzl's words became a reality fifty years later. For in 1937 the British government appointed a Royal Commission on Palestine before which David Ben Gurion expressed the historic right of our people to the Land of Israel, declaring 'The Bible is our mandate.'

Ten years later, the United Nations Assembly voted on 29 November 1947, by a majority of thirty-three to thirteen with ten abstentions, to recognise the existence of a Jewish State and declared Jerusalem an international city.

Finally, I want to refer to a vital question: 'What is the cause of Jewish survival?' We have seen that throughout the ages, Jews everywhere have been subjected to persecution, massacre and exile. How can we explain the miracle of Israel's survival? Mighty empires have perished but Israel, bleeding and lacerated, still lives on. The Prophets of Israel, in their eternal messages of hope and courage, tell the nation that no matter how dire the situation, suffering and exile will come to an end. As God's chosen people, the Sinaitic Covenant has not been abrogated and the bond between God and Israel still exists. It is this assurance that has kept us alive and made us worthy to witness the return of our people to Eretz Yisrael.

60

The Halachic View of the Relationship between the Individual and Community

B EFORE discussing the halachic implications of the individual's relationship with the community, it is necessary to consider the biblical and Rabbinic attitude to the sacredness of the human personality. In other words, how does Judaism define the individual as a person before considering his relationship to the community?

Hillel said: 'If I am not for myself, who will be for me? And if I am only for myself what am I?' (Pirke Avot 1:14).

In this famous declaration, Hillel the Elder expressed in one short paragraph a summary of Jewish philosophy: that of personal responsibility together with social responsibility; the duty one has to oneself and one's duties to others.

I believe that this teaching of Hillel expressed firstly a spiritual structure of Judaism, a fundamental principle in the sacredness of the human personality stamped, as the first chapter of Genesis teaches, that a human being is created in the image of God with a divine likeness, and it is important that he be constantly aware of this. The Psalmist expresses this: 'You have made him but little lower than the angels, and have crowned him with glory and honour.' (8:6)

The injunction to perceive oneself as created 'in the image of God' placed a duty on man not merely to enjoy the things of creation but to enjoy the sacredness of his life. It thus became the supreme duty of a person to acknowledge his role in life and make him aware that he is master of his destiny.

Commenting on the verse: 'After the Lord your God you shall walk' (Deuteronomy 13:50) the Sages in Gemara Sotah 14a ask: How is it possible for man to walk after the attributes of the Holy One, Blessed be He? How can mortal man imitate God's ways? But it means a person is called upon to imitate God by putting into practice his attributes of being merciful, gracious, slow to anger and pursuing truth. This concept of man's mastery of his life is best illustrated through the purpose of the mitzvot, the laws and regulations he must fulfil. By fulfilling the positive and negative commands of the Torah, it is as if a Jew declares: 'I do not possess unlimited authority over the things of creation but through fulfilment of the mitzvot bring about a state of sanctity in my life.'

It was this fundamental principle of the importance of the human personality that the Mishnah in Sanhedrin 4:5 asserts: 'God created a single man to teach that whoever destroys a single individual in the eyes of God it is as if he destroys an entire world and whoever saves the life of a single individual it is as if he had saved an entire world.'

But whilst the belief in the sacredness of the human personality is fundamental to Judaism, equally essential is a person's role in and responsibility to the community. Unlike ancient Greek and Roman societies where the 'state' or 'society' had a priority over the rights of the individual by its use of unlimited authority, Jewish law recognised both man's individual rights to self-preservation and duties to others.

The Gemara in Baba Metzia 62a tells the following story. Two men were travelling in the desert and one of them had a jug of water. If the owner of the water drank the water he would survive, but if both drank of the water, both would die. Ben Patura said: 'Let them both drink and let them both die, for it is said "And your brother will live with you"' (Leviticus 25:36) Rabbi Akiva said to him: 'No, "and your brother shall live with you", your life takes precedence over his'.

Whilst the Rabbis did not demand that one need sacrifice one's own life to save another, they did teach that it is one's duty to save the life of another. For commenting on the text: 'Neither shall you stand idly by the blood of your neighbour' (Leviticus 19:16), the Midrash states: 'From where do we know if one sees his fellow man drowning in the river or attacked by robbers or by a dangerous animal that it is one's duty to save his life?' The Torah says: 'Neither shall you stand idly by the blood of your neighbour' (Sifra). Of course, this only applied when it did not endanger one's own life.

Though human life was sacrosanct, yet life was not considered to be a personal possession to be destroyed at will. It was therefore forbidden for one to destroy his life even if it led to breaking a command of the Torah. It was only during the Hadrianic persecution in the second century that at a conference of the Sages at Lydda it was decided that a Jew forced to violate all the biblical laws might do so except for three cardinal prohibitions. These were *Avodah Zarah, Gilui Arayot* and *Shefichat Damim* – idolatry, adultery and murder (Menahot 99b). Except for these three transgressions which were considered the highest form of *Chilul Hashem* – desecration of God's name – a Jew could transgress a divine precept. The Tannaim of that conference based their ruling on the biblical verse: 'You shall keep My statues and My ordinances, which if a man should do, he shall live by them, I am the Lord' (Leviticus 18:5), that the law was given to live by and not to die by (Avodah Zarah 27b).

The Rambam, Maimonides, comments on this as follows: 'When it is stated to transgress rather than to be killed and a person prefers to suffer death rather than transgress, he is as if guilty of depriving himself of life' (Yesodei HaTorah 5:4).

The Rabbis, in recognising the inalienable rights of the individual, were also aware of the duties the individual had to the community. During the period when the Great Sanhedrin existed and during the period of the Babylonian Talmud, the rabbinical authorities appointed *Batei Din* – Jewish courts – in every city or town to control the observance of Jewish law. Furthermore, they established a central authority in Jewish communities to run the affairs of the people by a governing body of seven notable individuals. Through this body, the community would pay taxes, and sanctions were applied against those who violated the rules. By the Middle Ages, the concept of a '*kahal*' – a 'Community' – was established in which members were expected to adhere to the rulings of the community. '*Al tifrosh min hatzibbur*' (Pirke Avot 2:4) – 'Do not separate yourself from the congregation' became an established rule of conduct whereby the individual was called upon to take his responsibility within the framework of the community.

The Talmud states: 'When the Jewish community is in distress, let one not say: "I will go to my house and eat and drink and peace be upon my soul." For if one shows himself indifferent when the community is in distress and distances himself from their needs, such a person shall not behold the consolation of the community' (Ta'anit 11a). From this we see the great importance attached to community solidarity.

Our Sages placed great importance upon community solidarity and they understood that there were two types of individuals who did not wish to be part of the community. One was a person *'haporesh min hatzibbur'* that is, one who does not wish to identify himself with the community. The second was one *'haporesh midarkat hatzibbur'*, one who distances himself from the laws of the Torah and does not wish to be associated as a Jew. Whilst both separate themselves from the ways of the community, the latter is considered a heretic and has no share in the world to come. We thus learn how important the Rabbis viewed those who excommunicated themselves from the people of Israel.

There is an accepted teaching in Judaism that Jews are sureties for one another In Hebrew it is called *'Kol Yisrael arevim zeh bezeh'*. The Mekhilta of Rabbi Ishmael explains when the Jewish people stood at Har Sinai to receive the Torah, they pledged themselves to be responsible for one another. This principle of mutual responsibility placed a duty for one to help prevent any person from committing an offence be it tale bearing or committing a sinful act.

One of the unique aspects of the Jewish community was the attitude towards philanthropy. Tzedakah was not viewed merely as a religious duty but a legal responsibility to be enforced through the courts. As such, every community had a right to levy taxes that were enforceable by law. Maimonides explains this legal responsibility. He writes: 'Whoever does not desire to give charity or does not give as much as he can afford, the Bet Din can force him to give as much as they consider he can afford to give' (Matanot Aruyim 7:10).

This concept of individual responsibility was of course reciprocal. Just as the individual was responsible for the welfare of the community, so also was the community responsible for the welfare of the individual. Our Rabbis explain the verse 'And you shall be unto Me a kingdom of priests and a holy nation' (Exodus 19:6) that Israel is all one body and soul and if one sins his acts affect the whole nation and vice versa. According to this the community can be held responsible if they could have used their influence to prevent these acts.

Let us conclude with the following statement from Maimonides on the importance of the individual's solidarity with the community. 'If a Jew is not concerned with the suffering and distress of the Jewish community he excludes himself from the religious community in its totality and shows himself indifferent when they are in distress' (Hilchot Teshuvah 3:11). However, on a positive note the Gemara states 'whoever identifies himself with the needs of a community will be privileged to see its consolation and success' (Taanit 11a).

In this sketch of the statement of Hillel, we have seen a wealth of understanding, in his ethical teaching, of the great value one places upon his own life and on that of his relationship to the community.

61

Dead Sea Scrolls – The Discovery and Importance

Background

In the spring of 1947, a Bedouin boy named Muhammed Adh-Dhib was minding some goats near a cliff on the western shore (Judean plateau) of the Dead Sea. Climbing up after a goat which had strayed, he noticed a cave that he had not seen before and he idly threw a stone into it. There was an unfamiliar sound of breakage. Frightened, he ran away but later came back with other shepherds, and together they explored the cave. Inside were seven tall clay jars, among fragments of other jars. When they removed the bowl-like lids, a very bad smell arose, which came from dark oblong lumps found inside each of the jars. When they carried these lumps outside the cave, they saw that they (some according to Sukenik's diary) were wrapped in lengths of linen and coated with a black layer of what seemed to be pitch or wax. They unrolled them and found long manuscripts, inscribed in parallel columns on thin sheets that had been sewn together. Though these manuscripts had faded and crumbled in places, they were in general remarkably clear. The writing was not in Arabic.

Puzzled by the scrolls, they carried them along whenever they moved. In Bethlehem, they showed them to a Syrian merchant, who thinking that the language might be ancient Syriac, sent word to the Syrian Metropolitan at the Monastery of St. Mark in Old Jerusalem.

The Metropolitan Mar Athanasius Yeshue Samuel expressed a decided interest. He knew that nobody since the early centuries had lived anywhere near Ain Feshkla (a spring at the Dead Sea). When a scroll was brought to him at the monastery, he broke off a fragment and burned it and could smell that it was leather or parchment.

He recognised the language as Hebrew, but as he was not a Hebrew scholar, he could not determine what the manuscript was. He sent word that he would buy the scrolls, but in the meantime the Bedouins were off again on another expedition. Several weeks passed. It was July before one of the Syrians called to tell the Metropolitan that he and the Bedouins would bring him the scrolls. Following the meeting, the Metropolitan purchased five of the scrolls, along with a few fragments for a price rumoured to have been £50 (others say £24). Two of the scrolls turned out to be successive portions of one manuscript which had come apart and which Millar Burrow, Director of the American School of Oriental Research, entitled the 'Manual of Discipline'.

After purchasing them, the Metropolitan Samuel was faced with two problems: 1. To find out what the manuscripts were and 2. How old they were. He consulted a Syrian whom he knew in the Palestine Department of Antiquities and a French priest at the Dominican Ecole Biblique, a centre of archaeological research in Old Jerusalem, but he received no information whatsoever.

Eventually it seems that, by chance, a Jewish doctor, Dr M. Brown, called at the monastery to inquire about renting a building which was part of the church's property. The Metropolitan took the opportunity to ask him about the scrolls. He contacted President Dr Magnes of the Hebrew University, who sent two men from the University Library. They said that they would have to consult an authority on these subjects and asked to photograph a few columns of one of the manuscripts. Although the Metropolitan gave his consent, the librarians did not return. (This may have been due to either the troubled relationship at the time between Arabs and Jews or to the absence of Professor E. L. Sukenik, the university's Professor of Archaeology.)

In any case Professor Sukenik returned at the end of November and was told by another Jerusalem antiquity dealer (an American friend of his) that some manuscripts from a cave on the Dead Sea were in the hands of a dealer in Bethlehem. He bought the three scrolls on 29 November 1947, along with the two earthenware vessels in which the scrolls had been stored. Later he acquired additional parchments.

On 18 February 1948, the Metropolitan made contact through Butros Sowmy with the Acting Director, Dr John C. Trever of the American School of Oriental Research. Dr Trever investigated their age by comparing them with the Kodachrome slides of the Nash Papyrus.

'The similarity of the script in the papyrus and the scrolls was striking,'
he said. He copied out a passage from one of the scrolls and eventually
identified it as a part of Isaiah.

The Nature of the Find

Why were the scrolls hidden away in the cave? Probably in order to
prevent their profanation. Jews have long been accustomed to take such
precautions in disposing of holy books grown unserviceable through
wear and tear (Dead Sea Scrolls by Sukenik, p. 22) Thus, the tentative
opinion was that the cave had been used as a Genizah.

Another scholar, Professor Kahle, put forward the theory that the
cave was used to hide the scrolls away in time of religious or political
persecution. The very fact that the books were hidden with the utmost
care for their preservation, wrapped in linen and inserted into
earthenware jars, is a strong argument for his point of view.

Professor Sukenik felt that his theory was confirmed by the state in
which the surviving scrolls were discovered, both those acquired by the
Metropolitan Samuel and those in possession of the Hebrew University.
Thus 'the Thanksgiving Scrolls were not regularly rolled together (the
three sheets) and one of them was even shoved into the roll. From the
condition of the material it was clear that the sheets had not been
separated by the Bedouin in pulling the scrolls out of the jar, but on the
contrary the scrolls must have been put away in this state in ancient
times' (ibid. pp. 22–3). From the detailed account of the state of the first
Isaiah it appears that part of this scroll was already spoiled and worn
from overuse prior to its being hidden in the Genizah cave.
Furthermore, the main body of the scroll contains many corrections,
erasures and retracing of obliterated letters. Other scrolls are torn in
two.

The Isaiah Scroll in our possession affords still more conclusive
proof. Beyond question untouched by human hands, this scroll contains
isolated fragments from various chapters, with the continuous text
beginning only in Chapter 38. Moreover the fact that this scroll
conforms in both reading and spelling with the masoretic text would
seem to refute Kahle's theory that the scrolls were concealed because

they differed from the officially canonised text. In addition, 'the meticulous care accorded the scrolls by those who hid them away was explicitly required by tradition'. Thus in the Talmud it is said 'Rabba said: A Torah scroll which is worn out is to be buried near a scholar'. R. Asa bar Yaacob said 'And in an earthenware pot, as it is written, put them in an earthenware vessel, that they may last for a long time (Jeremiah 32:14)' (Talmud Bavli, Megillah 26b).

The Age of the Manuscripts and Their Importance

In order to understand the importance of the Dead Sea manuscripts, one has to realise that our earliest text of the Hebrew Bible, the Masoretic text – though it had probably been established as early as the beginning of the second century BCE – is no more ancient than from the ninth century. Before that, our main versions of Scriptures are the Alexandrian Septuagint, a translation into Greek begun around the third century and not finished until two hundred years later.

According to Professor Sukenik, in the words of Yigal Yadin, his son, 'the first scroll as the most ancient surviving manuscript of the prophet Isaiah ... that it was at least a thousand years older than the earliest previously known copy' (*The Message of the Scrolls*, p. 16) .

The scrolls found in the cave near the Dead Sea constitute the most important discovery made in the field of ancient literature. For the first time, copies of books actually written down in the days of the Second Temple have come into our hands, some of them biblical texts, others works of whose existence we hitherto knew nothing.

62

Moses: Man, Servant
and Prophet

THE BIBLE is full of a galaxy of great men and women who played decisive roles in the history of the Jewish nation, but Moses towers over them. What kind of man was he that the Torah says of him, 'There has not arisen a prophet in Israel like unto Moses'? (Deuteronomy 34:10)

In the opening chapters of the Book of Shemot, we read of his birth and early life. He was born at the height of the persecution of the Israelites in Egypt. Through Divine Providence, he was saved from death by the King's daughter who took pity on him and adopted him as her own son. He received the highest type of education as a member of the Royal family. On growing into manhood, he went out to see the suffering of his brethren and sympathised in their fate.

The Midrash states that he left the luxuries of the palace and went to assist them in their plight by preparing the clay for their bricks and assigning to them responsibilities according to their abilities. For example, the strong were given heavier burdens to carry, whilst the weak had lesser ones (Exodus Rabbah 1:27).

Tradition has it that Moses showed great compassion not just to human beings, but to all God's creatures. On one occasion he saw a small lamb running towards a pool of water. As it exhausted itself on the way, he picked it up saying, 'If I had known that you were thirsty, I would have carried you here.' A heavenly voice then called out: 'Surely you are fit to be a shepherd' (ibid 2:2,3).

Forced to flee from Egypt and live in Midian, the Bible hardly mentions anything of his life there. One does not know of his ambitions or thoughts, except that he married Zipporah, the daughter of Jethro the priest of Midian and tended to his flock. We are told that on looking after the animals, 'He led them to the farthest end of the wilderness'

(Exodus 3:1). Our Rabbis explain that he did this 'in order to keep away from robbery that they should not pasture on the fields of others' (Rashi).

One day in the wilderness he saw a flame of fire coming out of a bush which was not consumed. On turning aside to see, he had a 'revelation' of God calling out to him to become the leader and redeemer of his people. A number of reasons why Moses declined the offer are stated in the Torah.

He presented five reasons for this.

1.   Who am I to go to Pharaoh?
2.   When I come to Bnei Yisrael and say to them 'the God of your fathers has sent me unto you' and they shall say unto me 'What is His name?' what shall I say to them?
3.   'But they (the Israelites) will not believe me, nor hearken to my voice, for they will say, 'The Lord had not appeared to me.'
4.   'I am not a man of words...I am slow of speech and of a slow tongue.'
5.   'O Lord, send I pray by the hand of him whom Thou will send'.

It is only when God finally assured him of success by telling him that Aaron his brother would be his interpreter to Pharaoh and the Jewish people that Moses accepted his mission of confronting Pharaoh and performing the signs and miracles that would lead ultimately to the exodus from Egypt.

In the third month following their departure, the Israelites arrived at the foot of Mount Sinai where they received the Torah and entered into an everlasting covenant with God. Sadly however, shortly after this when Moses did not return to the camp after remaining for forty days on the mountain, some three thousand Jews worshipped a golden calf. Moses, seeing this on his return, destroyed this image and punished those responsible. He further shattered the two Tablets of the Decalogue below the mount.

On learning that the Almighty intended to destroy Israel and wished Moses to become the father of the nation, Moses displayed his love for them by interceding on their behalf. He said to God, 'And now, if you will, forgive their sin: and if not, blot me out, I pray Thee, out of Thy book which Thou hast.' (Exodus 32:32) In these words Moses showed himself as a loyal leader of the nation. His devotion and love for them meant that he was prepared to have his name removed from the Torah: 'For I cannot be a leader who failed to gain mercy for his people.' (Rashi). Here Moses revealed his true inner self, his fatherly character and deep affection for Israel.

The forty years of wandering in the desert were a period of constant tension and crisis. Time and time again the people complained. They wanted food as they were not content with the manna and complained of lack of water. They even threatened to appoint a new leader and return to Egypt. The bad report of the Ten Spies, the rebellion of Korach and the accusation that Moses was seeking greatness, undoubtedly lowered Moses' spirit. Yet with all this, it did not deter him from his love for them and his mission to lead them to the Promised Land.

Perhaps the greatness of Moses can best be illustrated by the offence his brother Aaron and his sister Miriam committed when speaking about the Cushite woman he had married. In his humility he did not respond. The Torah states,

'Now the man Moses was exceedingly humble, more than any person on the face of the earth.' (Numbers 12:3) Indeed, consumed by his self-effacement, not only did he not respond but he cried out in prayer: 'Please God, heal her!' (ibid. 12:13)

One can now understand that before Moses died, the Torah paid him the highest tribute given to anyone. Whilst during his life he was referred to as 'Man of God' (Deuteronomy 33:1), in death he was called 'Servant of God' (ibid. 34:5) and the greatest of all Jewish prophets. In the words of the Torah: 'Indeed, here was a man, a servant and the greatest of all Prophets who delivered our people from bondage, turned them into a Holy Nation and led them towards the Promised Land. Chag Sameach' (ibid. 34:10).

63

Haggadah

THE FESTIVAL of Passover commemorates the historical event of the liberation of Israel from Egypt. The Bible states: 'And you shall tell your son ... because of this the Lord did for me when I came out of Egypt' (Exodus 13:8). In Hebrew the word for 'you shall tell' is '*Haggadata*', teaching us of the duty of a father to instruct his child about the miracle that happened in Egypt.

The fascinating Seder service therefore dates back more than three thousand years. In the course of time, many additions were added to its present form. The Haggadah is an anthology of Jewish literature with quotations from the Torah, Mishna, Talmud, Midrash and poetry. Composed in many ages, it has become one of the most popular books in Jewish life.

The recital of the Haggadah is the essential part of the Seder Service. The narrative can be divided into three sections. First is the story of our early history where our ancestors were idolaters, our entry into Egypt as free people, our bondage and liberation from servitude. The second part relates to the command to eat the Pascal lamb (done in Temple times), the Matzah and the Maror. Finally, there comes the recital of the Hallel, hymns of thanksgiving and the promise of ultimate redemption with a return to Eretz Yisrael.

We commence the Seder ritual by reciting the Kiddush, attributed to the Men of the Great Assembly who lived during the Second Temple. This is followed by washing of the hands with Maror dipped in salt water (the Sephardim use lemon juice), a requirement mentioned in Pessachim 115a. The breaking of the Matzah in two and the hiding of part of it as Afikoman to be eaten at the completion of the meal is symbolically to remind us of the Pascal lamb which was eaten (during Temple times) at the conclusion of the meal.

The recital of the '*Ha Lachman Anya*' (this is the bread of affliction) is based on the phrase '*Lechem Oni*' in Deuteronomy 16:3

and is an invitation to extend to the poor to come and share our festival meal. It is composed in Aramaic, the vernacular of the Jewish people at that time, so that even the ignorant might understand it.

On four occasions the Torah speaks of relating the story of '*Yetziat Mitzrayim*' to our sons, each being mentioned with a different expression. From this the Rabbis deduced that the Bible refers to four different types of sons, each to be explained in a manner they will understand.

The drinking of four cups of wine corresponds to four statements found in Exodus 6:6,7. They are 'I will bring you out; and I will deliver you; and I will redeem you, and I will take you out.' The four cups of wine are then the four-fold divine promise of liberation. The fifth cup of wine, referred to as Elijah's cup, is not drunk and kept as a reminder of Elijah being the herald to the Messiah's arrival.

In the third century, there were different opinions between Rav and Samuel, two distinguished scholars, as to whether one should mention in the Seder Service the story that our forefathers were once idolaters or just mention that we were once slaves of Pharaoh in Egypt and that God delivered us. As a compromise, both texts are included in the narrative.

Following the washing of hands and recitation of '*Hamotzi*', the Maror is dipped in salt water (Sephardim using lemon juice) as a reminder of how the Egyptians embittered the lives of our ancestors. The recital of Hallel are songs of praise and express our gratitude to God. The Seder concludes with prayers of thanksgiving to the Almighty for the endless favours He continues to bestow on the House of Israel.

64

A Happy New Year

A T THIS SEASON of the year, it is customary to wish each other the popular greeting *Shanah Tovah* – a Happy New Year. The literal translation of the word 'Tovah' is 'good', yet instead of wishing one another 'a good New Year' we say 'a Happy New Year'. Perhaps the reason is that we associate the word 'goodness' with 'happiness', as our prayers for the New Year are centred around this idea.

Whilst happiness is an idea hard to convey, yet when we possess it, it is the greatest gift that God confers upon us. To our Rabbis, it is an obligation placed upon every Jewish person in the Torah. Time and time again, the Bible commands us to be 'happy'. 'You shall be happy', 'You shall serve the Lord with Joy', 'You shall be happy with all the good the Almighty has given.'

One of the ways to be happy is in the performance of *Gemilut Hasadim* – deeds of lovingkindness. It is through almsgiving and charitable acts that one imitates the Holy One, Blessed be He, and attains happiness. Indeed, every act of goodness is in itself an act of happiness and the way to be happy is to make others so. Rabbi Huna ben Hanina commented on the verse: 'After the Lord your God shall you walk'. Is it possible for a moral person to emulate the Divine Presence? Has it not been said: 'For the Lord your God is a consuming fire, yes a jealous God'? But you may emulate His attributes. Just as He clothes the naked, as it is written: 'And the Lord God made for Adam and his wife clothes of skin and clothed them', so you do the same. Just as the Holy One, blessed be He, visited the sick, as it is written: 'And the Lord appeared to Abraham at the grove of Mamre (following his circumcision), so you too should visit the sick.' The Holy One, blessed be He, comforts the mourners, as it is written: 'After the death of Abraham, God blessed his son Isaac', so should you comfort the mourners. The Holy One, blessed be He, buries the dead, as it is written: 'And God buried Moses in the valley'. So should you bury the dead (Talmud Bavli, Sotah 14a). The Bible thus teaches us that happiness can be achieved by virtuous living, by sharing and being of service to our fellow men.

Joyous prayer is yet another way of being happy. An Amora, Rabbi Ibu, emphasises the happiness one can achieve through devout prayer. He says: 'When you come before your Creator in prayer, let your heart be happy that you are privileged to do so conscious of standing before God' (T.B. Shabbat 30b). The Mishnah in Berachot 6:1-3 makes mention of numerous prayers of thanksgiving which we make daily, reminding us of the Almighty's goodness. When one recites the gifts for health, family life and thanksgiving for our daily existence, one establishes a close connection with the Almighty in a true spirit of joy.

Maimonides, speaking of the command 'love the Lord your God' in the Shema, writes: 'When a person contemplates (in prayer) God's great and wondrous works ... And a glimpse of His wisdom, one will immediately praise Him, glorify Him and joyously long to come close to Him' (Yesodei Hatorah 2:2). It is this expression of joy that Judah Halevi, the eleventh century poet and scholar said, in the Kuzari, with regard to prayer being to the soul what food is to the body.

Study of the Torah is yet another way of deriving true happiness. King David, in the Psalms, describes his great joy in this by stating: 'I rejoiced over Your testimonies as much as in all riches ... I occupy myself with Your statues, I will not forget Your word' (Ps 119:14, 16). Again, 'I will delight myself in Your commandments which I have loved ... And I will meditate in Your statutes' (ibid. 48). And again: 'O how I love Your laws! It is my meditation all day' (ibid. 97).

Rabbi Chaim Volozshin in his work 'Ruach' writes: 'When feeling joy, you will be able to gain more from one hour of Torah study than from many hours of studying when sad.'

The Chazon Ish, in a letter to a student, said: 'Physical pleasure can give a person some degree of happiness, but this cannot compete with the true feeling of happiness that one can derive when one toils in Torah learning.' A Happy New Year – where shall we find it? It shall be found in human kindness, prayer and the study of Torah. These are the ways to a truly good and happy life.

Shanah Tovah!

Bibliography

Bachya ben Joseph ibn Paquda (11th century) *Duties of the Heart.*

Burke, U. R. (1923/2011) *A History of Spain from the Earliest Times to the Death of Ferdinand the Catholic*, Charleton, SC: Nabu Press.

Kobler, Franz (ed.) (1953) Letters of Jews through the Ages. East and West Library.

Newman, L. I. (2012) *Jewish Influence on Christian Reform Movements.* Varda Books.

Philo (1st century CE) On the Decalogue, Vol. VII: On the Special Laws. Loeb Classical Library. Cambridge, MA: Harvard University Press.

Sukenik, Eleazar (1955) *The Dead Sea Scrolls of the Hebrew University.* Jerusalem: Hebrew University; Magnes Press.

Yadin, Yigal (1957) *The Message of the Scrolls.* New York: Simon & Schuster.

Biographical Notes

1. Saadiah Gaon. Ninth century. Greatest of the Geonin, Head of Talmudic Academy of Sura, Babylon. Philosophical work *Books of Beliefs and Opinions.*
2. Solomon ibn Gabriol. 1021–1058. Spanish philosopher and poet.
3. Rashi, Rabbi Shlomo ben Isaac. 1040–1105. Foremost of Bible commentators and greatest commentator on the Talmud.
4. Kuzari. Yehudah Halevi. 1080–1142. Spanish poet, philosopher and physician.
5. Rashbam. Rabbi Samuel ben Meir. 1085–1174. Grandson of Rashi. Explains Biblical texts in the plain natural sense.
6. Abraham Ibn Ezra. 1092–1167. Spaniosh grammarian, poet, philosopher and renowned Biblical commentator.
7. Bahya Ibn Pakuda. Eleventh century. Author of *Hobot Halebabot* ('Duties of the Heart').
8. Rambam. Rabbi Moshe ben Maimon, known as Maimonides. 1135–1204. Foremost medieval philosopher, physician and author of Jewish Code of Law *Mishneh Torah.* Also 'Guide of the Perplexed'.
9. Ramban. Rabbi Moshe ben Nahman. 1194–1270. Great Spanish Talmudist. Biblical commentator and mystic.

10. Bahya ben Asher. Fourteenth century. Commentary to the Pentateuch.
11. Hizkuni. Hezekiah ben Manoch. Thirteenth century. Bible exegete.
12. Akedat Yitzhak. Issac Arama. 1420–1494. Spanish Talmudist. Commentary to the Pentateuch.
13. Joseph Albo. Fifteenth century. Spanish philosopher and preacher. Author of *Sefer Ha-Ikkarim.*
14. Don Isaac Abravanel. 1437–1508. Spanish commentator to the Bible, philosopher and statesman.
15. Sforno. Obadiah ben Yaacov. 1475–1550. Italian Bible exegete and physician.
16. Or Hahayyim. Hayyim ben Attar. 1696–1743. Moroccan Biblical commentator and Kabbalist.
17. Luzzato. Rabbi Moses Hayyim Luzzata. 1707–1746. Kabbalist, poet and writer of ethical works.
18. Kedushat Levi. Levi Isaac Berdichev. 1740–1809.
19. Haketav Vehakablah. Jacob Zvi Mecklenberg. 1785–1865. Commendatory to the Pentateuch.
20. Rabbi Samson Raphael Hirsch. 1808–1888. German Rabbinic leader and defender of Orthodox Judaism. Notable writer and Biblical commentator.
21. Malbim. Meir Yehudah Leibush. 1809–1880. Russian scholar and noted Biblical commentator.
22. Torah Temimah. Baruch Epstein. 1860–1942. Commentary to the Pentateuch.
23. Avraham Yitzhak HaCohen Kook. 1865–1935. First Chief Rabbi of Israel.
24. Menachem Mendel Schneerson. 1902–1994. Foremost religious leader and Head of the Lubavitcher Movement. Wrote extensively on all aspects of everyday life.
25. Joseph Hertz. 1872–1946. Chief Rabbi of the British Commonwealth.
26. Samuel Belkin. 1911. Rabbi, educator, President of Yeshiva University in New York.